THE LIFE OF A PAINTER

JOHN LAVERY

THE LIFE OF A PAINTER

THE
LIFE OF A PAINTER

By

SIR JOHN LAVERY, R.A.

AN ATLANTIC MONTHLY PRESS BOOK

ILLUSTRATED

BOSTON
LITTLE, BROWN AND COMPANY
1940

Published May 1940

THE ATLANTIC MONTHLY PRESS BOOKS
ARE PUBLISHED BY
LITTLE, BROWN AND COMPANY
IN ASSOCIATION WITH
THE ATLANTIC MONTHLY COMPANY

PRINTED IN THE UNITED STATES OF AMERICA

To

ALICE

ACKNOWLEDGMENTS

My grateful thanks are due to Katharine FitzGerald and to John Stewart Collis for helping me to put my stray memories together. Also to Mr. Walter Shaw Sparrow for permission to quote from Cunninghame Graham's Preface to *John Lavery, His Life and Works.* And to the following who have kindly given me permission to quote from letters: –

Lady Cynthia Asquith and Mr. Peter Davies, Lady Raleigh, Mrs. Ormond, Mrs. Kevin O'Higgins, Mrs. Gertrude Parry, Miss Joanna Collins, Sir Alfred Cope, Captain Cunninghame Graham, Mr. George Bernard Shaw, Mr. Macaulay Stevenson, and Mr. Shane Leslie.

My acknowledgments are also due to the following who have kindly allowed me to reproduce pictures in their possession or of which they hold copyright: –

The Marquis and Marchioness of Londonderry, Emerald Lady Cunard, Mrs. McKean, the Earl of Harewood, the Earl of Lonsdale, Lord Melchett, Viscount Cowdray, Sir Patrick Ford, Bart., Sir William Burrell, Major John Spencer-Churchill, Mr. William Aitken, Mr. Thomas Lamont, Mr. Ossian Donner, Dr. Ronaldson, Mr. Richmond, Mr. Hugh Spottiswoode, Lady Duveen of Millbank, and the American Order of Hibernians.

Also to the following galleries: –

Aberdeen, Belfast, Buenos Aires, Dublin, Dundee, Edinburgh, Glasgow, Luxembourg, the National Museum of Wales, National Portrait Gallery, National War Museum (London), Uffizi Gallery (Florence).

BIOGRAPHICAL NOTE

John Lavery, born 1856. Member of the Royal Academy, the Royal Scottish Academy, and the Royal Hibernian Academy. Also of the Royal Academies of Rome, Antwerp, Milan, Brussels, and Stockholm, the Société Nationale des Beaux-Arts of Paris and the Autumn Salon. Is "*Hors Concours*" in the Society of French Artists and Corresponding Member of the Institute of France. Member of the Sécessions of Berlin, Munich, and Vienna and the Society of Spanish Artists in Madrid.

Knighted 1918. Chevalier of the Crown of Italy and of Leopold of Belgium. Hon. LL.D. of Queen's University, Belfast, 1935; of Trinity College, Dublin, 1936; and a Freeman of both cities.

CONTENTS

ILLUSTRATIONS

(AT END OF BOOK)

ILLUSTRATIONS

ILLUSTRATIONS

THE LIFE OF A PAINTER

I

THE FARM

In the official list of Members of the Royal Academy I see that my birth is recorded as in 1857, and not as recorded in the register of baptisms in St. Patrick's Church at Belfast, as 1856. For my birthday, to save explanations when asked, I chose St. Patrick's Day as being, for an Irishman, easy to remember.

No doubt my first years count — but I cannot account for them. Yet, as I remember climbing over trestles where barrels had been kept in a wine-and-spirit shop, it is evident that my father was a wine merchant. In considerable contrast to Ruskin's father, who was also a wine merchant, he seems to have sold out and cleared out at an early stage, leaving his wife and children to fend for themselves. My brother Harry would be about four; I three; my sister Jane two. We were divided up: Harry going to my Aunt Rose's father, a doctor; I to her husband, Edward Lavery, a farmer; and Jane to an Uncle Richard, a publican in Belfast. I do not know what happened to my mother. I am told that she died of grief when my father was drowned on his way to America.

The farm I was sent to was called "The Back of the Wood," and the farmer, Edward Lavery, my uncle, was a tall man with a kindly face, clean-shaven, and with a mouth that broke into a smile at the slightest provocation. He was unable to look severe when he was supposed to punish me, but he made pretense when my Aunt Rose pushed him to it – which she frequently did, on tiring of the operation herself. I can recall two such beatings quite distinctly, though there must have been dozens. I was now about six or seven, and the process was to bare a part of my body and apply a "Sally Wattle" with all the force at her command, making it painful for me to sit for some time afterwards. But those two beatings were especially painful, for on the first occasion I had outraged her sense of propriety and on the second her sense of economy. One day in the stack yard I had seen the men slip down from the stack they were building, crawl along the ground to an opening in a thick-set hedge, and make signs for silence. I followed on tiptoe and was privileged to witness a passionate love scene. In the kitchen, where the farmhands had their meals, I must have been asked to show what I had seen – and so great was my success that the loud laughter brought my aunt rushing down to carry me off for execution. The other occasion was after I had been sent to school with two half crowns in my pocket to pay school fees. As I ran, one of them fell out of my blouse into the ditch and was lost. Not knowing what to do, I spent the remaining one on sweets. The reckoning came all right.

Besides these evidences of refinement, my aunt showed her feeling for fashion by wearing the most striking crinolines and driving in the smartest jaunting car in the locality. Her father being an eminent doctor, she felt no doubt a step above her position. She made great changes to "The Back of the Wood," and when the railways began to appear in Ireland she renamed the farm "Train-View Moira." She had two sons and a daughter of about my own age, who were dressed with scrupulous care while I was given clogs and corduroys in the winter – though in summer I went barefoot, frequently coming to grief on the broken flints, thorns, and stubble.

Yet I remember very little of those days. I see myself sitting with someone in front of the fire, her feet on the fender and myself lying on the hearthrug kicking up my heels – until I kicked over a kettle of boiling water, the scar of which scald lasts to this day. I remember the excitement of being lifted on to the immense height of a jaunting car and tucked in with a rug, while a weeping woman – what woman? – embraced me. Then the image of a farmyard where a cart with a frightening load of hay, a mountain, jammed me against a gatepost, while a large orange wheel passed over a tin plate I had dropped in my terror. Next, trying to hold on when a horse put down his head to drink in a horse pond, but slipping headfirst into it. Finally, sleeping in a nursery with a girl of fourteen or fifteen who, much to my discomfort, kept embracing and fondling me in a manner that was anything but pleasant at that time – keeping me awake when I was in real need of sleep. Years afterwards I saw a coarse fat woman that I was told had been my nurse.

I was made a great deal of by the farmhands and called "the poor wee orphan" – terms which I did not quite understand but was prepared to profit by. I had also other companions, for I went to school, a Protestant one though I was a Catholic, where I was subject to jibes about the Pope and Holy Water from the other boys. In County Antrim, Cromwell had seen to it that Catholics were cleared out and their place taken by "planters." Every Twelfth of July bands of Protestants paraded the countryside, the booming of their big drums terrorizing the Catholic children, making us feel that our last hour had come. It was not till long afterwards that I learnt that religion had nothing to do with the demonstrations; they were politics camouflaged to suit the mob. Evidently my parents had understood the policy of keeping quiet. I inherited that discretion, and am a great hand at lying low when in a minority.

However, I must not forget the trees and the woods of "Train-View Moira," and the joy I often got lying on the ground looking up through the leaves and drinking in the wondrous colors. I believed that when the great cumulus clouds took strange shapes in the summer they were God and His Angels, and I ran and jumped along the road when alone, thinking I was there with God, sometimes kneeling down to pray in a state of ecstasy, then bounding into the air as if I were flying – all in sheer *joie de vivre*. This was all brought about by perfect health and a missionary priest at school, who instead of telling us of the fires of Hell dwelt on the beauties of Nature.

THE FARM

When I was ten my aunt suddenly told me that she was going to send me across the sea to a very rich cousin of hers who had a big house with solid golden balls hanging over the front door. For days I dreamed of a fairy palace, and soon the day came when I found myself sitting in the cabin of the Belfast–Ardrossan passenger and cattle steamer. I had never seen the sea before, nor waves rolling up a beach. We arrived at the other side in early morning and proceeded to walk the mile or so towards our destination, which was at a place called Saltcoats. We passed two girls disporting themselves in the water, both of whom I painted forty years later. I was told that they were ladies of title from the big house close by, Montgomery Castle. It did not fulfill my idea of a castle. I was still dreaming of the Palace with the Three Golden Balls where I was going to live.

We came to our destination. We reached the castle. And looking up I did behold the golden balls. But the castle was a house upon the portal of which these words were written – UNION LOAN OFFICE. A pawnshop.

II

THE THREE GOLDEN BALLS

SUCH was my introduction to the land of Burns – Ayrshire. My experience of it, while interesting, was lacking in the poetical. My uncle had a remarkable clientele of sailors, negroes, and miners, who came to pawn a strange assortment including picks and shovels, guitars, banjos, concertinas, queer-looking knives and pistols, not forgetting a large Holy Bible and Foxe's *Book of Martyrs*, – highly illustrated, – which I was told not to look at. I liked handling these things, but I was especially taken with some tins of blasting powder and a page boy's livery. I remember the latter, because when my uncle was away I used to sneak out as a page boy and think no end of myself in the borrowed plumes. The blasting powder had a strong appeal, and on one Twelfth of July, being a Papist, I sought to gain favor with the other boys who were of the opposite persuasion. We damped little pyramids of powder and forced them into the "toories" of our "bonnets," and then, setting them alight, ran round yelling at the top of our voices. One fell off and was going out when there were screams for "more pooder." I rushed up with the canister, which immediately exploded so violently that the neighboring windows were blown to pieces, though by some miracle none of us were blown up — till we got home.

Traveling theatres came to the town, performing in large tents, admission from threepence to a shilling, where such plays were given as *Leah, or the Jewish Maiden's Wrong*, and *Ingomar, the Son of the Wilderness*, over which I shed tears. Known as the "wee pawn man," I used to hang about and get into the good graces of the artistes by giving them an old sword or dirk from the shop. The lady who played Leah held me in bondage until one day I saw her behind the scenes drinking porter out of a broken jug, the liquor escaping down the side. And on hearing her remark to some men, "There's that bloody boy again," I was cured and transferred my attentions to Mary Ann, who was the queen of "Paddy's Castle," a house in a back street where the sailors used to go with girls. Mary Ann was a dazzling blonde of about sixteen with an impediment in her speech — using Gaelic and hardly any English. She was mauled about by drunken sailors, and had great attraction for me, now getting on to thirteen. Owing to her reputation I dared not be seen speaking to her. But one evening when there was a crowd, she among them, trying to get into the theatre, I plucked up my courage and sidled close to her, whispering, "See you when we come out." She winked and said nothing. That was the beginning of my first attempt at love-making. Alas, it was about Easter time and I had to go to confession. There was no escape. It was not so bad as I had expected, but for a long time

I was not allowed out alone after dark. Although I knew that the Confessional was secret, I could not help thinking that Father Halloran had been talking to my uncle. Anyhow, I never saw Mary Ann again.

Besides bringing me these experiences the pawnshop enabled me to help my brother Harry, who suddenly turned up. He had been sent by Aunt Rose's father to a training ship at Plymouth. Dressed in his naval rig he was now on leave, but determined to desert. I fixed him up with a suit of clothes from the pawnshop. Having made a neat bundle of his discarded uniform with a heavy stone inside, we walked into the mining district to a disused shaft down which we threw it. We were terribly frightened and for a long time afterwards did not know what might happen. Getting well away from the pit shaft, we parted, Harry going off into the wilderness with the few shillings remaining from his leave money, intending to hide underground as a pit boy. Almost a year later a letter from him in a disguised hand let me know he was driving ponies in a pit at Longriggend, a name I have never forgotten. When he thought it was safe he came back to Glasgow and took a job as a clerk in the Glasgow Corporation, where he remained twenty years, got married, brought up and educated two sons and a daughter. Then one morning, without saying anything, he walked out and was next heard of in Australia, years later, where he eventually died leaving a will in favor of the wife and family he had deserted.

It may have been this meeting with my spirited brother, or merely the exuberant inexperience of youth, that made me suddenly decide to make a change! I cannot remember where I got the money, – I must have robbed the till, – but one morning I took train for Glasgow. In a low part of the town I found lodgings where there was a boy a trifle older than myself, in sailor rig, whose company I had for some time. He went about the country with others similarly attired carrying packs. They were known in town as "Dry Land Sailors," because they sold wares consisting of gaudy junk supposed to have been brought home by them from their last voyage, though as a matter of fact they were merely peddling the shoddy trash they had picked up in Glasgow. At times I was a little in doubt as to the wisdom of keeping company with them and their girl friends. Their language was new to me, not to mention their freedom with each other. However, soon my money ran out and I was forced to take French leave of the lodging – though I left an empty bag to ease my conscience.

When I began to feel hungry I thought of going to a pawnshop, but had a peculiar aversion to being seen in such a place. I went round looking for one in some obscure corner, but when I found it my courage failed me. Seeing another boy idling about, I showed him a large cameo pin that I was wearing and told him that if he could get half a crown on it I would give him sixpence, explaining that I did not like going in myself because the man knew me. He took it and disappeared up the stairs. I waited, but he did not return. I crept up into the lobby and peeped into the half-dozen boxes only to find, in the language of the locality, that I had been bilked. It cured my diffidence.

For a whole week I was without board or lodging. It was summer, and I slept on benches in Glasgow Green, wandering the streets and back yards in the darkness, picking up food that had been thrown away, and washing it in the fountains when the daylight came. Actually, I think it must have been longer than a week, for they say that I was a skeleton when found wandering one night in the Saltmarket, and brought back to Saltcoats.

Just then there happened to be an outbreak of smallpox, which I naturally caught. I was immediately segregated and placed in an attic with an Irish "Sairey Gamp," whose treatment, I expect, was homely. When the crisis was over and I could see again – I had been blind for a week – she tied my hands so effectively to prevent my scratching that I escaped without a mark. She explained that the only safe disinfectant was whiskey baths for a couple of weeks after I was supposed to be better. This suited her. She had an orgy until she overstepped the mark and was dismissed.

The whiskey baths couldn't have done me much good for my next recollection is of standing naked in the theatre of the Glasgow Royal Infirmary surrounded by a dozen medical students with two doctors explaining that I was an interesting case of hernia, varicocele, and some other diseases that I cannot recall the name of. After much incomprehensible talk I was put in a ward for observation, where I remained about a week, having constant visits from doctors and students until it was decided that I should be operated upon. The other inmates of the ward frightened me by telling me that I was to be taken to the dissecting room and cut up. A nurse took pity on me, and after much persuasion secretly got me my clothes and I slipped out with the visitors on visiting day. I do not know what happened to the nurse, but she was so popular with the other patients that I felt sure none of them would give her away.

Once again I was back at Saltcoats, and then over the water to "Train-View Moira." Strange as it must seem, there was then talk of making a priest of me. The idea came from my uncle, but my aunt luckily did not see me as the perfect candidate for Holy Orders, so I found myself back in the fields herding the cows once more.

Hunger was my chief feeling. I can remember how, when my aunt had a tea party, I would be sent across the field to O'Hara's grocery store to get a couple of baker's loaves, the bread baked at home on a griddle not being stylish. I would pull them apart and eat as much as I dared. Mrs. O'Hara sometimes gave me a ginger biscuit or barley sugar. I had a fierce appetite and could devour anything — raw turnips, carrots, all kinds of fruit in quantities — and not feel ill, but still hungry. I enjoyed the usual food of the farmhands — buttermilk, oatmeal porridge, wheaten bread and butter, eggs and bacon, potatoes *ad lib.*, and occasionally, when a calf was killed, veal. During Lent the fare was very strict – porridge with cold water and sugar, boiled potatoes and turnips, wheaten and oatmeal bread and butter, no milk, and on Good Friday no food of any kind. Nevertheless I grew in health and strength. A butcher was called in when the slaughter of the pigs was necessary. This was done when the children were at school. Once, however, I saw him at work, and the horror of it remained with me for years and prevented me from indulging in pork.

Every genuine artist creates the circumstances necessary for his fulfillment, and unconsciously does the right thing at the right time. Hence in spite of the good food, and the security, and the experience of what I had been through when I ran away before, I was determined to get away again. A certain boy I had known in Glasgow had told me that it was always possible to get something of a job in the Mineral Department of the Glasgow and South-Western Railway. I made much of this to my uncle and aunt, and was so successful that without further inquiry they let me go off with five pounds in my pocket. On the way I spent most of it in entertaining a cousin at the theatre at Belfast and having our photographs taken, so I arrived in Glasgow with the proverbial half crown and my belongings in a carpetbag. Pat McLoughlin, the friend in question, found me sitting in his lodgings when he came from work. I told him what had happened and he behaved nobly, going out and bringing back a couple of kippers and a steaming loaf from the baker's. I can remember with what gusto I devoured my share of the food and the excitement of my first music hall afterwards, where we looked down from the gallery at the flamboyant chairman surrounded by beer-laden tables and hilarious company listening to the great Macdermott sing: —

> Oh, the sea, the beautiful sea,
> Oh, that up and down motion [with gestures],
> When on the lee scupper
> One lays one's supper,
> It's, oh, the beautiful ocean . . .

followed by other artistes with "Champagne Charlie" ("After the opera is over, After the opera is done, We gems of the very first water, With the ladies we'll tootle-tum-tum") and such-like ditties, McLoughlin joining in the choruses with the rest of the house. I felt on the high-road to fame and fortune, for it was the happiest evening up to that time that I could remember.

The next day I did manage to get a job with the Mineral Department of the Glasgow and South-Western Railway, which was in a back siding with hundreds of coal trucks being shunted backwards and forwards outside the window. My job was to take their numbers and weight of contents and enter the details and make out the total for the day. I am still pretty helpless with figures, and I used to sweat blood trying to add up the long columns. In the little office or box where this was done, there was a clerk in charge who allowed me considerable freedom after the first day and did not bother to correct my columns, though he could do in a minute what had taken me hours.

Soon this work drove me distracted and I decided to give it up. Then, realizing that in this case I would immediately relinquish my wages of 7s. 6d. a week, – which with an occasional sovereign from my uncle was all I had, – I decided to carry on till my month's wages were due. I knew that with the best will in the world I could not make the monthly returns, so I looked up the ledger for the returns of the other months and struck an average, which was accepted. I then took my wages and disappeared into the blue, with a sense of shame and remorse for what would be sure to happen when the report reached the auditors – for my friend and chief would certainly be dismissed.

Pat again came to my aid. I was anxious to get out of Glasgow at once, and owing to him I got a job in another pawnbroking business in Hamilton, which is a garrison town a few miles out. I arrived on Saturday. Unfortunately on Sunday afternoon a Scots Grey from Belfast invited me into the barracks. He had two girls with him. They were both domestics from Mount Vernon, and in the evening I was weak enough to promise to see them home, some eight miles away. It was a clear frosty night as I walked back, but I became very tired and, brushing the snow off a low wall, sat down. About four in the morning I was awakened by a pitman going to work. I had been frozen asleep for about five hours, but managing to crawl on for another mile to the pitman's house, I lay down on the floor in front of the fire. On arriving at the pawn office I discovered that the rush was over, since Monday morning in a pawnshop is the busiest in the week, and consequently I was dismissed by the infuriated pawnbroker.

There was no alternative but to go back to Glasgow, and I made for a low quarter of the town called "Gallagate" or the Road to the Gallows. This place consisted of dilapidated mansions that once had housed the aristocracy but were now inhabited by the poor. They were turned into the meanest lodginghouses, where a cracked sign indicated that single beds could be had for sixpence a night and double ones for fourpence. It was to one of these mansions that I found myself forced one cold and wet evening towards midnight. The half-open door, hanging at a slant from a broken hinge, led to a broad staircase lit by a gas lamp in the street. The interior was strewn with rubbish and dirt from which there rose a strong smell of disinfectant. As I reached the top of the stairs an argument was in progress between the lodging-house keeper and a drunk who, after a display of foul language, was finally ejected by being thrown down the stairs — taking me with him. On reaching the top of the stairs again in the semidarkness I heard a harsh voice calling out, "And what the hell do you want?" Taking care to show him by my demeanor that I was at least sober, and rattling the few coppers in my pocket, I resolutely said, "I want a bed" – hoping that he would not turn me out when he found I wanted only half a bed. My finances could not run to a whole bed to myself, for I had the next day's meal to think of and was already very hungry.

I entered what, at one time, must have been a magnificent room, for even now the gold of the elaborate cornice glittered in a shoddy way. There was a great open fireplace dismantled even to the grate, and on the hearth was a blazing coal fire surrounded by small tin cans of a more or less uniform size, their owners squatting on the floor or on anything they could find. The furniture consisted of empty boxes. When I had time to observe the inmates I saw that they were all of the usual navvy type, ranging from sixteen to sixty, mostly smoking and talking. The only light came from the fire, and in distant corners I could discern shadowy forms sprawling on the floor seeking rest, while an extra-loud snore would occasionally eclipse the conversation round the fire. The squalor was sickening, and I was wondering whether I would be able to stand it when I was brought to my senses by the keeper with, "Weel, ma lad, where's yer money?" "Could I have the share of a bed?" I asked. For a moment I thought he was going to turn me out into the street; but after relieving himself of some unprintable oaths he thought better of it, saying briefly, "Oot wi' yer fourpence." With the aid of a bit of candle guttering down the side of a bottle he preceded me into a still more grimy room. Packed together on the floor and on mattresses raised from it were ten or twelve human forms, all with some kind of covering and a sort of bolster under which the sleeper had clearly put his valuables. Taking me to a most unsavory-looking object stretched on its back on a mattress in a gloomy corner, my host said, "There ye are, ma wee man, ye'll be as snug as a bug in a rug." I winced at this pleasantry a little, as I could see he was speaking from long experience. His parting salute was, "Put yer trousers under yer head." In the semidarkness of the night the full horror of the place was less evident than in the morning light, when most of the laborers had gone to work, leaving behind only the lowest of the low, smelling to heaven. My bedfellow was still there. In the window there was a sink called a "jaw-box," with running water but no soap or towel. I washed as best I could and dried myself with the back of my waistcoat.

When I went out into the street I met a friend. He was three or four years older and had been my ideal of everything I thought wonderful. He could draw in a way that thrilled me, and besides other accomplishments was an athlete and a boxer. On one occasion I remember holding his jacket and keeping an eye out for the police while he gave a lesson to a drunk who had bumped against him in the street. While we had breakfast I told him where I had spent the night. He told me he had enlisted the day before in the 60th Rifles. Although I had a genuine horror of service in any shape or form, my admiration for him was such that I hurried off to take the Queen's Shilling.

Fortunately I was disqualified.

III

PROGRESS AND TRAGEDY

I RECORD these seemingly unimportant early episodes in my life since they played their part in guiding me to my goal. After my failure in the Mineral Department and my fiasco as pawnbroker's assistant, culminating with my horrible experience in the doss house, it became increasingly clear to me that I was not and never could be a jack-of-all-trades. Moreover, I had a particular admiration for anyone who could draw, and even a faint hope that one day I might be able to draw myself. Thus when my uncle heard of my condition from Pat McLoughlin and demanded that I should go back to school at Saltcoats, I was now quite ready to comply.

That this was the turning point in my life is proved by the fact that no sooner had I got back than I became fascinated by the grocer. Not because he was a grocer, but because he drew profiles in pencil that held enormous interest for me. I used to copy them by placing them against the window and tracing on another paper. From then on I disfigured anything I could make a mark on until I was getting a reputation almost equal to that of the grocer. I even went to the length of trying to draw full-face.

Till then I had never seen anything in the way of painting except gaudy lithographs of the "Battle of the Boyne," and oleographs of the "Stations of the Cross" and others of a religious nature. One day I won in a church lottery an oil painting magnificently framed in gold, said to be a wonderful likeness of the late Cardinal Bono. Unfortunately my uncle would not let me take it out of the convent to which it belonged, on the grounds that it had been blessed by the Pope. However, in lieu of this he gave me a golden sovereign, saying that he was sure that when I became an artist I should be able to paint a cardinal for myself.

To this day I remember that scene. I recall the way my uncle said it. I cherish the first words of encouragement I had ever known. They fanned my imagination; they liberated my energy, they caused me to draw day and night – gaining confidence with every step I took.

Then one day there appeared in the *Glasgow Herald:* "SITUATIONS VACANT – A smart lad with knowledge of drawing wanted. Apply with specimens of work to J. B. MacNair, Artist and Photographer, 11 West Hill Street." I dashed for the first train to Glasgow and was taken on as an apprentice at £10, £15, and £20 per annum for three years. I had read of the Old Masters taking pupils, and it was with feelings that Raphael might have envied that I got back to Saltcoats with the news. My uncle forgave everything, rigging me out in new clothes and saying that one day I might be a great artist with people in carriages coming to my door.

Above all, I could now at last afford the Art School. My first lesson occupied two hours, drawing straight lines and curves, the second outlining a vase, the third in copying parts of the human face, and so on until a certain proficiency in what was called "drawing from the flat in outline" was attained. Then the cast and two whole years grinding at it, the life class, and a sense of being on the road to fame and glory.

So here I was in Glasgow again – a different person this time. My age was about seventeen. I soon conceived a great admiration for MacNair, for he was not only a good artist on canvas but a better one on flesh. One day two visitors who did not look at all like sitters called and asked for him. I was about to tell them that he was not at home when they said that they had come to be painted. There was a distinct smell of stale alcohol about them, and I observed that each had a black eye, not to mention some disfiguring gashes. It struck me as strange that they should choose the morning after the night before as the most propitious time to have their portraits painted. I soon learned, however, that they wanted their actual faces painted. This was immediately carried out with great skill by MacNair, who was able to remove all traces of nocturnal excess by means of oil paint. In an hour's time a Romeo and an Orlando left the house.

This time I chose a more respectable lodging place than the Road to the Gallows. My landlord and landlady were a road mender and his wife. He was a quiet little man who was always tired when he came home from work;

and I remember how his front teeth were gone, causing his pink chin to project, while his pipe, which never remained alight, hung loosely from his gums — a depressing spectacle. My landlady was one of those wives who cause the puzzled onlooker to ask the question, "How did he ever come to marry her?" Her aggressive and truculent air, her large nose which hooked at a dangerous angle, her formidable jowl which supported some very large hairs, the cast in one eye which always remained stationary no matter how much the other revolved, were intimidating. As befitted the severity of her countenance, she was a devout Presbyterian and would have no truck with Papists or the "Scarlet Woman" of Rome — though at that time I missed the full significance of her changing the sex of His Holiness. If she caught me drawing on Sunday she did not fail to assure me that no good could come of it. However, as she went to church from eleven till two and from three till six, I could still get in six hours' work.

I did not have all my meals with her, for I managed to attend the Art School at this time, and regularly had some of my meals at the Cooking Depots of Glasgow, which were organized to supply the working classes with good wholesome food at modest prices. Breakfast cost fourpence, dinner eightpence. For the former one got a bowl of porridge and cream, a roll, butter, and a large cup of tea; for the latter one got minced collops, potatoes and vegetables, stewed rhubarb or rice, often Scotch broth — a meal in itself hard to beat. And this food was of better quality than one finds in Soho or most other places for which fantastic prices are charged compared with my fourpence and eightpence.

These depots were run by women, principally girls from the country, many very pretty Scottish lassies – a Scottish girl must always be called a "lass" – with frank, bright honest eyes and wonderful complexions, free from the art of Elizabeth Arden (not that I would for a moment deny her gracious talent). The first time I went in I was served by one about sixteen, called Jean. And after that I never missed going to her table. The trouble began by my cashing in on the word "artist," which then, as now, excuses the commission of sins. She was thrilled with the romance of it, and saw to it that I got the best of everything in the pot, and much bigger helpings. It is difficult for me to-day to call it by its right name, but I was in love and intended marriage and everything was fair. Soon I took her to be photographed at MacNair's studio, I sitting on a papier-mâché rock and she standing by my side with a hand possessively on my shoulder, with a distant view of the Clyde on a painted screen in the background. She had on her Sunday frock for the occasion, and I a fashionable short-tailed tweed suit buttoned up to the neck, showing tie and cameo pin. My thumb was in my trouser pocket, slightly drawing back the coat that I might display my silver watch and chain. MacNair remarked: "Ye're in for it noo, John."

I think this photograph rather put me off. And when one Sunday evening she asked me to come and see her people and I heard myself prayed for during family worship as "the stranger within oor gates," I began to cool off. I began to make excuses about other invitations, and sometimes I would not see her for a couple of days. She looked very sad, but did not complain. I noticed at times that her large brown eyes with long lashes were inflamed. It did not occur to me what the real cause was. I thought she had some inflammatory disease and that her beauty was going. She saw I was wavering.

A new girl had come on the scene, straight from a boarding school, with superior manners and of good family. I behaved like the cad I was and without shame turned my attention to the beautiful blonde. I tried to impress her by showing her my drawings; and with the idea of proving to her that I was going to be a great artist I visited a traveling phrenologist, who for five shillings offered a printed chart of the formation of one's head, showing for what one was best fitted in life. I could not afford five shillings, but I was entitled to a verbal statement for one shilling – which I took. It was not entirely satisfactory. Feeling my skull with the tips of his fingers, he asked me questions which I have forgotten, my answers undoubtedly giving him a lead. His diagnosis was: "With education you will reach great heights. Without it you have the capacity for reaching criminal depths. As you are neither educated nor uneducated you will not disturb the world." I was so disappointed with this recommendation that I nearly forgot to ask him what profession I was fitted for. He asked to see my hands and then said I would pass as a typesetter or printer's devil. Thinking over the result afterwards, I felt sure that had I paid five shillings it would have been very different; anyway I felt confident that the nitrate of silver that stained my fingers, and which he had obviously mistaken for printer's ink, had prompted his decision as to my most suitable profession. If the phrenologist did not help me, he at least opened my eyes to that form of humbug, including palmistry.

The new girl, Georgina, had flaxen hair parted in the middle with pigtails emphasizing an exquisitely formed ear such as Leighton would have delighted in, while her large eyes were blue and, like her lips, a trifle protruding. She called me John, though up to that time I had usually been called Jock or Johnnie. John sounded important; besides, it was sweet the way she pronounced it in her Glasgow accent with a fascinating lisp. She was a showroom girl at MacNair's, and I was so enamored that, though a Catholic, I found myself sharing a hymnbook with her at evening service in a Presbyterian Church. I tremble to think what Aunt Rose, who had brought me up and taught me sufficient Latin to serve at Mass and make the correct responses, would have said.

I gave Georgina Moore's *Irish Melodies* and other sentimental works preparatory to proposing. She married a man with a beard and was the subject of one of my first paintings, entitled, " 'Tis better to have loved and lost, Than never to have loved at all."

I doubt, however, whether I felt the loss of Georgina

very keenly. I was so obsessed with the mystery of art that had suddenly come to me. Nothing else mattered. At the bottom I cared only for my work. The reader may think that I say this with satisfaction. Perhaps I do – in relation to the girls in the depot, Jean and Georgina. It is with neither satisfaction nor complacency that I think of Jane – my sister. When I could afford two rooms and a kitchen to myself, Jane, who was now sixteen, came to keep house for me. She was very proud of the position, and washed and scrubbed all day and every day until the place shone like a new pin. As I was at the School of Art night and morning we saw little of each other except on Sunday, when we went to early Mass that I might have a long day for painting.

My sister felt lonely at times but I scarcely gave her a thought. One day I noticed that she had been weeping. She said it was nothing, but I began to be uneasy and to pay more attention to her. I saw she had quite changed from the bright laughing girl who had arrived to a listless creature insisting there was nothing wrong and assuming a hollow gayety. This went on for some weeks until the obvious truth could no longer be hidden. The shock was terrible. Looking back on all that happened, I cannot understand how I could have been so cruel. I try to make excuses on the ground of my youth and my all-conquering ambition to be a painter, but I can never forgive myself for the tragedy that followed. We had very little money to live on, but as everything seemed to be running smoothly I never troubled to ask her if I gave her enough each week for household expenses, and her pride would not allow her to ask for more. Instead she had been pawning the few bits of jewelry she owned, and had thus become friendly with the pawnbroker's assistant, who, without my knowledge, had been visiting her in my absence. When he discovered what had happened he disappeared.

When I found that he had gone to America I at once set about sending her after him – not knowing where she would find him, nor realizing what it meant in her delicate state of health, nor what a steerage passage really was! One idea absolutely absorbed me, and one only – to get her away before anyone should know of the disgrace and I be involved.

It was raining when we reached the docks, and I can still see that horrible den, steaming with its stench of humans, tar, and bilge water deep down in the fo'c'sle of the very small Anchor liner as she lay close to the Broomielaw Bridge in Glasgow; nor shall I forget the mass of men, women, and children huddled together in the semidarkness, intensified when the only source of daylight was obscured by the emigrants struggling down the ladder with their soaked bedding and other belongings. Only bare wooden boards were provided for sleeping accommodation. I left her there and returned to the empty house. Feelings of remorse come to me when I remember her frightened look of anguish, with no word of complaint when we said good-bye!

She found him. Though he had run away to America

to escape it, he married her and the child was born. In a few months they returned to Glasgow. I was shocked at her appearance, now strange and wild-eyed. I went to see them from time to time but I could not like him, though he had made good. He was educated and talked advanced socialism with which neither my sister nor I had any sympathy. Another baby came. She was unhappy and careworn. He was hard and coarse in appearance. I stopped seeing them, blaming her for the mess. She knew that I was ashamed of the connection and appealed to me for help to escape from him. One late evening I found her waiting for me outside the studio door, afraid to knock. I refused to help her.

Two days later her husband came to tell me that she had thrown herself over Stockwell Bridge into the Clyde, and that I was wanted at the police station to identify the body. She looked young and beautiful with the strange serenity of death.

The terrible tragedy had shaken me, but uppermost in my mind was the thought of how I could hide the fact that I was in any way connected with it. Fortunately her married name would appear in the papers and not mine, thus sparing me questions by everyone who knew me, my name being so uncommon in Glasgow. I knew I was wrong and tried to ease my conscience by going to confession, but the knowledge of my miserable want of courage and affection haunted me for years – and haunts me even as I write these lines.

I doubt if there is a more heartless crew than poets,

painters, and composers. We are encouraged in this callousness by our lay brethren. I often wonder why. Robert Louis Stevenson said that we are merely on a par with the daughters of joy who are paid for doing what they enjoy most. Art is so sacred the love of it covers a multitude of sins, and so we excuse ourselves.

IV

SCHOOLS – GLASGOW – LONDON – PARIS

LET me pass — not retreat, I hope — from this aspect of my conduct as a man to my life as an artist, and outline briefly the evolution of my work during those early years: the years in the life of a painter or writer upon which all depends, the hours of labor, devotion, expectation, and unbounded hope.

I painted my first picture in 1876, when I was twenty. A woodcut of the "Death of Chatterton" appeared in a magazine about that time. It affected me very much and was the cause of my very first attempt at a picture. I was helped by the brother of my landlady, who was a copperplate engraver and knew a little about drawing, showing me how to square it off on a larger scale. I spent many months stippling it in water color, and when finished I thought it good enough to offer for sale. The difficulty, of course, was to find a buyer; but a raffle was suggested and tickets were issued at half a crown each. After the frame and the drinks all round had been paid for, I realized eight or nine pounds. Before the final draw the picture was on view in the bar parlor of a friendly publican, a patron of the Arts, which included boxing.

This initial success led me to attempt the Georgina picture mentioned above. It was a highly stippled water color, inspired by reproductions of Millais's "Yes!" and "No!" I spent a year on the picture and sent it to the R.A., priced one hundred guineas – sentiment is valued highly when one is young. It was rejected. Then to the Glasgow Institute of the Fine Arts, reduced further in price, to meet the same fate.

In the School of Art I made the acquaintance of a fellow student whose father had a furniture shop on the island of Islay. McTaggart, the great Scottish painter, when he was young held exhibitions there, and my picture was included in one of these. Then at long last for the first time I saw my name in print in the two-page catalogue. When the exhibition opened I bought the local newspaper, the *Glasgow Herald*, the *Scotsman*, and others, expecting to read long articles on the exhibition, more especially on the discovery of a young genius, myself. Armed with half-a-dozen papers I could not wait until I got home to my lodgings, and yet was ashamed to be seen reading them in public because I felt sure that everyone would know who I was and what I was looking for. I found a quiet corner in a back yard and went through every page, even the advertisements, without finding any mention of the show. To-day to be ignored is not so painful as it then was.

However, a year later, in 1879, I made an entry into the Glasgow Institute with a picture in oils called "Pious Reflections," which adorns these pages. Judging from the accuracy of the drawing I must have got help from the photograph of a girl in the same position.

After my three years' apprenticeship as a miniature painter over photographs on ivory was up, I took a small flat in a tenement house in the west end of Glasgow with a brass plate on the door, JOHN LAVERY, ARTIST, at the same time taking another engagement with another photographer at £100 a year. At the end of that time he desired to renew the engagement at £200. I thanked him but did not accept. He was not pleased and his parting shot was, "Well, ma man, ye may want to come back before lang, but mebbe I'll no want ye."

Then, carrying on as a free lance, I had my first experience of painting portraits from the life. An old dandy, a Papal count, hearing that I was Irish and a Catholic, gave me my first commission, which I tried to do without the aid of photography, because I was anxious that he should not think me a photographic colorist, particularly as he already had a number of colored photographs of himself, and terrible things they were. I struggled along for a couple of months, and in the end he was delighted with the result, for I had not failed to emphasize the signet ring on his little finger, bent with rheumatism, which he pushed well forward.

My studio was next door to a sentimental house painter who had given up his job and taken to painting portraits. One was called "Tender and True," a commission he had obtained from a newly married couple. In spite of the fact that it is most unlikely it was either too true or too tender, they did not appreciate it and refused to pay. One morning I met him climbing up the stairs, his face swollen and battered out of recognition. "Hello, Tommy!" I said. "What's the matter?" "A was oot collectin' ma account late yestreen, an', b' God, I had to fight for it."

In those days in Glasgow the existence of the artist's model was made known by advertisements in the *Herald*, which brought forth all kinds of applicants for the post. One morning I found sitting at the studio door a ragged, barefooted child of about seven or eight. "Would you be wanting a model, sir?" "Have you been sitting?" "A wus sitting to Rattray." Her reply indicated a familiarity with the profession that was surprising. Mr. Rattray was a stained-glass painter and I inquired what she had been posing for. "A wus posing for an angel, and he gave me saxpence an oor in ma claes and ninepence in ma skin."

She compared favorably to the girl who came to pose as Marguerite for a picture of the garden scene in *Faust*. She was terribly upset when "Faust" got a bit familiar in the greenhouse that was being used as a dressing room. She rushed out and refused to let him near her. Faust was a hussar that I had got from the barracks close by. She was very refined in her appearance and genteel in her choice of language. She would not pose again, saying to her friends, "I would not have went if I had knew."

Sitting at dinner one afternoon in the house of a friend, we heard a loud knock on the front door and a strange voice in the hall wanting to know if Lavery were there. A burly Highland policeman entered the dining room, looked hard at me, and said, "Are you Lavery?" "Yes," I answered with some anxiety. "Weel, ye're gutted." It was his delicate way of breaking the news that my studio had been burnt to the ground and my first masterpiece, " 'Tis better to have loved and lost," had gone with the rest of my belongings.

I cannot remember ever feeling so happy. I was insured for £300. At the moment I could not pay my rent, long overdue, and my present sitter, a busy city man, had got tired of sitting for his portrait. On the morrow he was giving me my last sitting, and I was in a terrible mess as I knew I could not possibly finish it. I had pawned everything I could get money on, literally my shirt, for food. I met with much sympathy, even from people who did not like me, and it was difficult to hide my joy at the thought of getting £300, a larger sum than I had ever had before.

It gave a brother brush an idea, and he had his studio insured at once. Shortly after, a gas jet attached to an easel was unfortunately left alight and burnt a hole in the canvas he was engaged on. He made a claim to the insurance company, and an inspector was sent round to estimate the extent of the damage and asked some searching questions, looking all over the place making no comment. As he was going out of the door my friend anxiously asked how much he thought he would get. The answer was brief — "About six months."

This good fortune put enough money into my pocket to pay my bills and let me go to London to attend Heatherley's Art School, in Newman Street. I remained there for twelve months – the loneliest year I have ever spent in my life. Every morning I walked from Liverpool Street Station and back in the evening without meeting a soul I knew. For a whole year, for all the communion I had with my fellow men, I might have been in the middle of the Gobi. In the school everyone went his own way when the classes were over, in the well-known English manner. The cheap lodgings at Dalston, with a dismal landlady who had recently lost her husband and was continually telling me how hard a struggle it was to make ends meet and how she never thought she would be reduced to taking lodgers for a living, were not a great attraction.

Yet to-day I hasten to add that no place I have lived has had the appeal of London, or its freedom. Cromwell Place has been my home for forty years without my knowing my next-door neighbor, and it has a call for me that no other corner of the globe has been able to give. At times I am pleased to leave Town, but I am always delighted to get back. Whistler dedicated his *Gentle Art of Making Enemies* to "The rare few who early in life have rid themselves of the friendship of the many." One can be of the rare few more easily in London than in any place on earth – the city above all others where a double life is possible.

Soon I began to feel that I should never be able to

make much progress at Heatherley's, and that only in Paris would I get the grounding that I needed. And, still owing to that windfall from the insurance company, I was able to do this.

This first journey abroad was slightly complicated by the fact that though I only took one suitcase I also had to take a lunatic. It was this way. About seven or eight years after the Franco–Prussian War I was taking lessons in French from a former *franc-tireur* who had escaped from Metz when that city capitulated, and come to Glasgow. His name was Gravet; his father, he said, was mayor when disaster came. When I knew him he was married to a pretty little Irish girl, the daughter of an Irish R.M. My French lessons were being given for a portrait I made of him and his wife. I well remember the strange look in his eyes and the hopeless misery of his expression at times. He gradually lost his reason, making it necessary to place him in an asylum, and hearing that I was going to Paris for the winter session at Julien's studio, his father-in-law came over from Ireland to ask me to take charge of the harmless lunatic on his way to Charenton.

Gravet's brother was meeting us in Paris, and it was arranged that I was to meet the father-in-law at Victoria. The rush of the Underground proved too much for his slow habits, and he was left standing on the platform at Charing Cross while the lunatic with his luggage and without a ticket was carried around the Inner Circle. Meanwhile all the different stations were notified that a man without a ticket might attempt to pass the barrier.

We waited until the train had had time to go round the circle twice without a sign of the traveler before we called in Scotland Yard. Next afternoon a message was received from Bromley, Kent, that a man answering the description had been found asleep and partially clothed on the side of the road outside that town, and at that moment was in bed in the workhouse there. How he had passed the ticket collector or where his luggage had gone remained a mystery.

We got him back to London and more clothing – he had only shirt and trousers, his boots were gone – and off we started for Paris by the Newhaven and Dieppe night boat. He was now in my full charge and, feeling tired, sleepy, and anxious, I suggested a comfortable seat in the saloon. I soon found it difficult to keep awake, so, pretending it was for warmth, I sat close up to him, slipping a bit of his overcoat under me, and went to sleep thinking I had made escape difficult. I woke a couple of hours later still sitting on the tail of his overcoat, but he was no longer in it. He was found right forward, stretched full-length on his face, a frozen mass, all but gone, gazing at the waves breaking against the bow.

His brother met us in the morning at the Gare Saint-Lazare. We three, with two stern-faced men, had breakfast together at the Grand Hotel. Poor Gravet, looking hopelessly unhappy, anticipating disaster without knowing in what form it might come, sat refusing to taste a morsel. His brother and the two strangers talked a great deal, not paying much attention to either Gravet or me until they rose from the table saying that it was time to go. The hotel bus took us to the asylum at Charenton, Gravet sleeping most of the way. We drove into a courtyard and were politely escorted into an office where doctors, warders, and others kept us for some time. The brother, Gravet, and I were then asked if we would like to see the place, and we went out into a wide passage, followed closely behind by three sturdy warders. We had not gone far when Gravet was suddenly pounced upon and rushed through a door at the side that was quickly barred. We were told that we might look through a grating and see him. There he was, walking quietly with the warders in a large sunlit courtyard. I was allowed to visit him on Sundays until the end came, some months afterwards, from softening of the brain.

On arriving at l'Atelier Julien I was asked by the *Massier* if I were English. I said, "No, Irish." "Are you a landlord?" "No." "How many have you bagged?" I was surprised to find him so well informed.

My first instruction was from Bouguereau. After he had looked at my drawings from the nude and asked me a number of questions he was very brief though kindly: "*Mon ami, ça c'est comme bois; cherchez le caractère et les valeurs.*" During the three winters I spent *chez Julien* I cannot remember being told anything else. The rest of my training came and continued to come from what I saw rather than from what I heard. But that does not alter the fact that we foreigners were getting our art training from what we believed to be the greatest French artists, and the nominal fees we paid merely covered the rent of the studios and the cost of the models. I believe at l'École des Beaux-Arts no charge at all was made. As a result, when we sent to the Salon we looked upon it as our right, and if our works were neglected or badly treated, all we had to do was to notify our special professor and the difficulty was rectified. The State purchased irrespective of nationality; all of which was very different from the treatment of the foreign artist in this country at that time.

The arrival of a *nouveau* was celebrated with rum punch and brioche, supplied by himself at a cost of twenty-five or thirty francs. One *mi-carême* a hundred francs were spent on an inauguration resulting in more hilarity than usual, and the *Massier* on a high stool, holding his glass aloft, in a deep voice as if in church, began, "*Esprit Saint descend sur nous,*" ending with "*Allons donc, messieurs, allons donc au Grand Numéro!*" I had not the slightest idea what was meant until I was told that *Grand Numéro* was the daytime indication of a licensed house for women recognized at night by a red light. The *nouveau* was raised shoulder high, and we sallied forth singing and shouting into a cul-de-sac where, sure enough, we found a *Grand Numéro* on a board above an ironmonger's shop. The number was 0609. Translated, it read "*Aux Ciseaux Neufs.*" Some were disappointed, I among them; having read the *Maison Tellier*, I was quite excited at the thought of seeing it in reality. "*Quelle blague!*" was yelled as we returned more boisterously to the *atelier*.

Coming from the Glasgow of that time I was delighted to see the pleasure we gave to the people on the street, who entered wholeheartedly into our buffoonery, making way for us everywhere, even the guardians of the law joining in. How differently such a display would have been treated at home! "Disorderly conduct whereby a breach of the peace might have been caused" would have been the charge. The French have the tradition, of course. I shall always remember the noise of the *atelier*, each student trying to bang and yell louder than his neighbors, singing sacred and bawdy songs, giving wonderful imitations of High Mass being chanted to profane music and blasphemous ritual. Up to that time I had been what is called a good Catholic, and an Irish one from Belfast to boot. I must say I was shocked and gladly joined my friend Alexander Roche, who attended the students' Mass every Sunday high up in one of the towers of Saint-Sulpice. But the ridicule had entered my soul, and it was not many months before I began to find the padre of Saint-Sulpice tedious and his sermons dull. By the following winter I had forgotten about him and had almost become an optimistic agnostic.

Wet or dry, Sundays were spent in the open, usually on the banks of the Seine in the neighborhood of Meudon. One Sunday, attracted by a pear tree in blossom, I entered a garden to make a closer study. While I was in the middle of my sketch the owner of the garden, very irate, asked what I meant by destroying his pears. Thinking that he might be demanding compensation, and as I could see no harm in what I was doing, I broke out at once into the most foul argot of the studio, with which I was much better acquainted than with the language of the Saint-Germain quarter. The poor man was so shocked and surprised that he ran away. I suddenly realized that I had not been accused of walking over his pear blossom, but over his peas, which had just been planted there, so I rushed after him. He thought that I intended to add injury to insult and ran faster. Pursuing him across the fields, I at length caught him up and, offering him a five-franc piece, explained my stupid mistake. He was quite nice and roared with laughter at the foul language, which he could now see I had been using like a parrot.

One Sunday I went to Nogent-sur-Marne and started a little canvas, which found a place on the line at the Salon next to the "Bar at the Folies-Bergère," by Manet. Mine was called "Les Deux Pêcheurs" and was purchased by Saint-Marceaux, the sculptor, for three hundred francs. On Varnishing Day a very chic little lady in the height of fashion, Marie Bashkirtseff, in front of whose picture "Pas Mèche" I had been standing, introduced herself, speaking perfect English, and congratulated me on my exhibit and l'Atelier Julien — where she also was — on having such a distinguished student. I am sorry to say that that is all I remember about her. At that time I knew nothing about her famous diary, in which she confessed her ambition and declared her will: "I swear solemnly — by the Gospels, by the Passion of Christ, by MYSELF — that in four years I will be famous." Years later I learnt that this qualified her for the rank of unwomanly woman in the eyes of W. T. Stead, who declared that "of the distinctively womanly there is in her but little trace. She is the very antithesis of a true woman." Actually I did not notice that.

Perhaps it was my ignorance of the language. The reader, before he closes this section concerning my early days in Paris, may feel that I have deplorably little to say about the French names which have since become famous, such as Monet, Pissarro, and Cézanne. The explanation is that I cannot learn languages. And if I could have learnt — as no doubt I could under severe pressure — there was little stimulus, owing to the fact that we foreigners kept together so much by going to the same cafés and rarely meeting any of our French *atelier* friends except at exhibitions. Our days were so completely filled up from eight to noon, from one to five, and from nine to ten in the evening, that little time was left for anything except sleep. I must say that very few of my countrymen show much aptitude as linguists, and it has always struck me as surprising that to-day they are so bent on adding to the already high and toppling tower of Babel, thus sending many an unhappy young man out into the world carrying a dead language when he might have a living one — all to please some men of theory in power.

After my success in the Salon my work at Julien's gained interest for my fellow students, especially the French, but this language difficulty made me appear dull and ignorant. This was no doubt a great disadvantage, and though I owe much to my French masters and have been glad at all times to remember them and pay them homage, I dare say I should have learnt more and been more influenced by the influential and impressed by the Impressionists. Yet in my own case I harbor doubts about this. I am not a man of theory, and no one ever knew less why he did what he did than I. I question whether artists themselves can gain by theory as much as critics. It may well be dangerous to know too clearly what one is doing, just as a lover is apt to lose rather than gain by too close a knowledge of his psychological reactions.

My happiest days in France were passed in the colony outside Paris at Grès-sur-Loigne, an inexpensive and delightful place sheltering not only painters but an occasional writer – R. L. Stevenson had just left when I arrived – or musician. One day a German girl, with the lovely name of Derka Rosen, arrived and caused some stir. Not because of her nationality, – she spoke French and English without an accent, – but because she had advanced ideas on art and life. She rented a large house which had not been lived in for years. Then a personality arrived: a rather delicate, sensitive young man called Delius who went to live with her quite openly, and as a matter of course took it for granted that young people of the opposite sex should live together if they so pleased. Later Derka became his wife. The garden, which ran down from the house to the river, was completely shut in and became an ideal open-air studio for models, which Derka put to great use, making it a small and very select nudist camp which would have been a complete success if it had not been for the mosquitoes.

Their arrival was followed by that of George and Louis, two American brothers who may claim an entry here by virtue of their originality, however ridiculous. They came from a mining camp out West. One had fallen in love with an American opera singer, Madame Nevada, who had been severely censured by a French dramatic critic. News of this had reached the brothers in their mining camp, so they packed up and made direct to the editor of the journal, carrying with them a case of pistols. After considerable trouble in finding the villain, they burst into his private room, planted the pistol case on his desk in front of the astonished critic, and pointing furiously from it to him and to themselves shouted, "Madame Nevada – duel!" After some time the purport of their mission was made clear by an interpreter, and they were informed that according to the French code of honor certain formalities had to be gone through before a duel to the death would be permitted to proceed. The time and place had to be decided, the presence of seconds and a doctor provided for, and, most important of all, the challenged had the choice of weapons. The Frenchman chose rapiers; George and Louis thought better of it and no duel took place.

They came to Grès to learn painting and were soon famous for the song they sung concerning Abraham Brown and the Maiden who was not wisely but too easily seduced from the narrow path – George singing Abraham Brown in deep bass and Louis acting as the Maiden in a high falsetto. It should be added, however, that George showed a certain aptitude for profundity as a critic, and a well-known artist of the day, Weldon Hawkins, owed at least one success to a criticism advanced by George. Hawkins had done an enormous canvas in the forest. Two peasants, a boy and a girl, had posed for him, and the title of the picture was "Young Lovers." When the work was framed and on the eve of being sent to the Salon, Hawkins gave a party and invited a number of us to wish him luck and to criticize. It was here that George came forward and suggested that in view of the fact that the young lovers were looking so miserable it would be better to call them orphans. This trifling alteration was made and the affecting picture was accepted with acclamations by the Salon jury and purchased by the State. The *Figaro* and other journals combined to congratulate the artist on the dignity and pathos depicted with such true insight. At the *Vernissage*, collectors gathered round him ready to purchase anything he might have in the studio.

All went well for a year and then the demand for his work became less pressing. Soon there was no demand at all and something had to be done about it. A brilliant idea occurred to him. He would visit his tailor, achieve as opulent an appearance as possible, go to Paris, visit all the dealers to whom he was unknown in person, especially in his present rig, and ask to see work by the famous Hawkins in his latest period. . . . "If Monsieur could wait for a few days they were sure they could get some." . . . He rushed back to Grès in time to meet a revived market, which, however, did not last long when the supposed patron did not turn up as he had promised.

Louis distinguished himself by not painting the old bridge. It was a favorite subject. I should think every painter who went to Grès introduced it in some shape or form. I did it on at least ten occasions. One that caused a good deal of talk was purchased by the trustees of the Carnegie Institute at Pittsburgh, and Lavery's "Bridge at Grès" became known in America. Years later an American dealer, wishing to pay me a compliment and at the same time show himself familiar with my work, said, "I think, sir, you are perhaps the best-known British painter whose work has reached the States. There sure is no picture more talked about than the beautiful Irish girl's portrait, 'Bridget Gray.' "

V

QUEEN VICTORIA – THE FLOWER GIRL – WHYTE

After my return from France my first successful picture was the "Tennis Party," which was accepted by the Royal Academy. It is generally considered – and I think fairly – that this picture expresses my debt to French teaching. Although I had only seen Bastien-Lepage on one occasion on the Pont des Arts, where I was presented to him by a fellow student, I had never forgotten his advice on figures in motion. Pointing to people passing, he said: "Always carry a sketchbook. Select a person – watch him – then put down as much as you remember. Never look twice. At first you will remember very little, but continue and you will soon get complete action." From that day on I became obsessed by figures in movement, which resulted finally in the "Tennis Party" and drew attention to what became known as "The Glasgow School." When it first appeared it shocked the critics. They lamented that so promising a young man, who had hitherto shown such good taste and high-mindedness in the choice of subject, should now decline into mere vulgarity. After the Academy it went to Paris and was bought for the Neue Pinakothek, at Munich. After the

War it was sold, along with a number of other foreign works, and now is in the Municipal Gallery of Aberdeen.

My next big effort was "Mary Queen of Scots." I am not particularly fond of history and have seldom been inspired by the past. As a rule, I am only happy with the visible object in front of me and have never been able to cope with poetry or music – though for some years I kept up a pretense of liking music and of knowing something about it, thus getting myself into many situations both embarrassing and boring. Yet from the first day I held a paintbrush my mind was made up to paint a great picture of the Scottish Queen, and I spent some years reading up the subject. I chose that part of the story where Mary wrote her plea for that pity and that mercy which at all times are pleaded for in vain – "*Je suis en piteux estat non pour royne, mais pour gentill-fame; car je n'ay chose du monde que ma persone comme je me suis sauvée.*" I concentrated on two scenes, the night and the dawn after the Battle of Langside when she attempted to reach Dumbarton Castle, accompanied by the faithful Lord Herries and a few other followers. I decided that this should be treated somewhat after the manner of Bastien-Lepage, everything *en plein air*. The French and Belgians praised the pictures, and the Flemish Government bought "The Night after the Battle of Langside" for the Brussels Museum.

The preliminary studies took me a long time and to many places. One very cold evening in a keen east wind

I was working, while a couple of peasants stood beside me looking on. The cold was too much for them, but before walking away the woman looked into my face. I saw her shake her head and heard her whisper to her husband, "Poor man." She thought I had escaped from the lunatic asylum a short distance off. But the farm servant who had been told to supply me with horses became quite interested in the work, especially in the study I was making of the Queen. After some hesitation one evening before leaving, he said, "Man, I would like it fine if ye would do a wee bit landscape of the wife."

I took great trouble with the accuracy of this picture, getting hold of genuine period armor before finding anybody to get into it. And it certainly was a job to get a model into it, for the average soldier is bigger to-day than he used to be. The model I got for Lord Herries in the "Dawn" picture was called Stuart. He was an idle, good-for-nothing fisherman who had more time on his hands than he could deal with. His father and he owned a derelict fishing smack left high up on the beach of the Gareloch by the spring tides. Whether it was not worth the trouble of getting her afloat or they were too lazy I do not know. I found them one day drying themselves in the sun after casting their nets; when the tide was low the son waded out until he was up to his neck and then dropped the net, bringing the rope back to the shore. At high tide they hauled the nets in with the catch. When I told him I wanted him to pose for Lord Herries, the only faithful adherent the Queen had left save for a few men-at-arms, he seemed to know all about it. The Stuarts will never be forgotten in Scotland.

His Lordship had a terrible time with the midges getting under his armor as he sat on his restive steed, cap-a-pie, late on a summer evening. In spite of this, and the extreme difficulty of getting into the armor, he was so proud of the part he was playing that he did not seem to mind. One day he fell over with a rattle. I rushed to him, got his helmet off, and found that his face was purple, his eyes staring, and his tongue sticking out. He had slowly choked. I filled the helmet with water and dashed it on his face. He soon recovered, and when I asked him why he had said nothing, he replied, "I wanted to bear it."

He felt he was protecting his Queen.

"Mary Stuart" was a very beautiful Irish girl whose name was Bella Cullen, the daughter of a coal miner. She had no education at all, but she might have been the Queen, her bearing and manners were so perfect. One bitterly cold day towards the end of the sitting she caught a chill. Six months later I went to her funeral. While she was ill I visited her. The squalor and dirt of the room in which she lived with her father, mother, and two sisters was appalling. There she lay in what is known as a "concealed bed," really a hole in the wall hidden by a ragged curtain, covered by a dirty, smelly blanket, her beautiful auburn hair literally alive with lice. There was a sickening smell of bedbugs, the room reeked with stale drink, a paraffin lamp gave little light and much smoke, the father home from the pit was dirty and dripping, there were snow and sleet outside. Yet when her cough would let her, a wan smile would suffuse her face of an angel, as she accepted it all without complaint. If saints are made by sacrifice and suffering she is one.

In the early spring of 1888 I held a small one-man show in Glasgow, and included in it were a series of sketches I had been making in the Glasgow Exhibition grounds. This led to my being chosen by the Glasgow Corporation to paint the State Visit of Queen Victoria, in August, for which £600 had been earmarked to meet the cost. Thus at one swoop I was ushered into royal circles, having up till then aspired to nothing higher in social life than the Lord Provost.

There was tense excitement in Glasgow on the day itself. From where I was perched on the side of the dais on a very small platform, looking through a hole in the curtain that screened me, I could only see the Bath chair being wheeled in, the bowing courtiers and the privileged ones who surrounded the chair where sat the stout, elderly lady, wearing a widow's bonnet and looking rather severe. Everyone bowing to the ground was my first impression. A movement of the curtain caused her to look in my direction; her glance seemed to penetrate the dark material and expose me and my paintbox. For the moment I was disconcerted and my hand trembled, but I managed to jot down a few notes of value. "Eddie" – now Sir Edward – Marsh admired the painting, so I gave it to him. I was surprised forty years after to find it in an exhibition of the Contemporary Art Society.

No one dared to ask the Queen to give a sitting, even in the Scotland she loved. The Lord Provost sent me to Sir Henry Ponsonby, her private secretary. He was very nice, but the best he could do was to give me permission to make a copy of Her Majesty's portrait by Von Angeli, her favorite painter. I could not very well tell him that a good untouched photograph would be better to work from than a painting by an artist, however good, because while a painting expressed the opinion of the artist, the photograph expressed no opinion at all and gave me solid fact. Besides, a sitter's favorite portrait in nine cases out of ten is sure not to be a likeness. When you come to think of it, how much more valuable as a record of fact a photograph of Christ would be than a painting by the greatest portrait painter that ever lived. I explained that there was no portrait of the Queen in Scotland painted from life that I knew of, and I feared that a copy of the portrait might not satisfy the people that had given her one of the most enthusiastic receptions of her reign. Perhaps he might consider putting my request before the Queen. He said he knew it would be useless. I tried the Honorable Harriet Phipps, the Duchess of Buccleuch, and Lady Southampton, all in special favor, but without success. At last, when I had given up hope and was prepared to depend on the camera, Prince Henry came to my aid; the Queen could refuse him nothing. He came to Glasgow with the royal entourage, and while he was giving me a sitting at Windsor I told him of my difficulty. He at once said, "I will ask the Queen." He left the room and returned in a few minutes. "The Queen will come at two o'clock." I got my things together and waited. On the tick the door opened and in walked a little lady followed by two ladies-in-waiting, all in black with their bonnets on. It was a very cold, large room with a very small fire in the distance, no other heating. The Queen looked warm, having a dark red complexion and plenty of clothing; the ladies seemed afraid to raise their voices. I offered the Queen a chair, which she refused, saying that she would rather stand. She asked what view of her face I wanted. I said, "Profile, if it please Your Majesty." She said she had put on the bonnet she had worn in Glasgow, at the same time looking me up and down; then she went on talking with her ladies. The subject of their conversation was flannel underclothing, which must have given the ladies some comfort, they were looking so cold. I might have felt embarrassed had I not had an important task on hand, the painting of the Queen. My anxiety to get it down blotted out the subject for the time being.

Before I could complete my study she indicated that she had had enough – about twenty minutes it appeared to me – and turned and left the room without showing any interest in what I had done. However, I was more than pleased that I had got something to show. Looking at her profile I was reminded of a Roman coin showing a Caesar.

In order to do the thing properly it was necessary to have over two hundred portraits, all of them painted from life. The difficulty was to get people to sit. But after the sitting from the Queen everything was plain sailing. The first of the distinguished throng to give me a sitting was Sir William Thomson, afterwards Lord Kelvin. At that time, September 1888, he was deeply interested in wireless, and explained to me how he was able to receive and send messages through the air without the aid of a connecting wire. I wish I could remember what he said as to the method, but, alas, only the broad fact that he was able to do so remains; besides, I doubt if I would have understood the technicalities of the explanation.

For my London sitters my friend Whyte lent me his studio on Primrose Hill. My first, after the English royalties, was Sir James Ferguson. Looking worn-out, he remarked by way of explanation, "That complete ass, Hamilton, kept me in the House until five o'clock this morning with his damned Home Rulers." The day following, Lord Hamilton came, and seeing the sketch of Sir James said, "I see that you have that old fool, Ferguson."

I went to Darmstadt. The Grand Duke had time to sit on a Sunday only. I told him that if people in Scotland knew that I had painted him on the Sabbath day they might not allow his portrait to go in the group. He replied, "Ah, you are very droll in Scotland. I found that one might play the organ and not the piano on that day."

Of all the royalties that I have painted the one that

stands out is the Princess Alix of Hesse, late Empress of Russia, because of her great beauty. I had been given a large reception room in the *Schloss* for a studio. The first morning, I well remember, I woke with a blinding headache, a prevalent trouble of mine, usually meaning a day in bed. It was the morning that the Princess was to sit, and I forced myself to go to the studio where a huge coal fire at either end was banked up. There were large hairy rugs in front. It was most fortunate that I arrived early. I was no sooner there than one fireplace was in flames and then the other. I was alone, there was no means of calling servants, so I rushed about, finally getting help — the whole staff with all sorts of fire extinguishers. It was astonishing how quickly everything was put in order; half an hour afterwards, when the Princess came in, no one would have known that flames and volumes of smoke had filled the room so recently. Even the air had been reconditioned. The Grand Duke was so pleased with the little study I painted that he asked me to come back to Darmstadt to paint a life-sized portrait of his daughter before she became Czarina. I have often regretted that I did not do it. She hypnotized me by the strange sadness of her eyes, like one on the verge of insanity yet sane enough to realize it. I shall always remember the look almost of terror that came and went as I was painting her.

The German royalties treated me with great deference, I presume because I was a foreign artist. In Germany in the eighties the status of a painter was equal to that of a general in the army; he was covered with decorations at public functions and saluted as a person of distinction. Times change.

When the whole picture, a canvas 10 feet by 8 feet, was completed, I took it down to Windsor to show the Queen. She said I had made the head too big for the body, and Princess Louise, the artist of the family, thought that there was too much foreground of red carpet; otherwise the work was considered successful.

When I was returning to Glasgow that night, Mr. Walter Wilson, a town councilor and the William Whiteley of Glasgow, came into my sleeping compartment and offered me £1000 a month for the loan of the picture for six months to exhibit in his establishment, preserving the option of withdrawing from the contract after the first month. He promised to send me the first installment of £500 on the morning after our arrival, which he did. When the Corporation heard of it, a meeting of the Council was called to have the agreement canceled. Part of the arrangement with the Corporation was that I should have the loan of the picture for a year, but it was not anticipated that I would have Her Most Gracious Majesty exhibited in a haberdashery establishment at sixpence a head. After the first month Mr. Wilson withdrew from the contract, having paid the second installment of £500.

One day while I was engaged on this Royal Visit picture an incident occurred which altered my life. Coming out of an artist's color shop in Regent Street early one morning I saw a young girl with a bright red shawl round her head like a gypsy, in a neat navy-blue frock, standing under the Arches rather shyly holding a little basket of flowers that she was evidently offering for sale. I was so struck by her extraordinary beauty that I turned back and asked her to let me paint her. She understood at once, and in the most charming manner said that she would. I had no card, but by good luck I had a letter from Windsor Castle in my pocket giving my address in Whyte's studio, which I thought would impress her favorably. I gave it to her and asked her to bring it when she came to sit in the morning. She was, I thought, greatly relieved at my confidence and more sure than if I had given her a card. She came to the studio the next morning looking happy and contented at the thought that perhaps, after all, there was something less alarming in an artist's studio than being stared at by passers-by in Regent Street – though fortunately she had not been there more than ten minutes when I spoke to her.

Whyte was bowled over by her and, I admit, so was I. She told us that she was eighteen, that she had run away from a convent school, and that her name was Kathleen MacDermott. Her appearance and accent suggested that she was Irish. I learnt years afterwards that she was seventeen when I met her, and her real name was Annie Evans, for she had taken her mother's name to prevent discovery. I asked her if she would care to come to Scotland to be an artist's model. She jumped at the idea, and a day or two after, Whyte saw us off at Euston by the express train bound for Glasgow. I got her lodgings, but within a year she developed a cough I did not quite like. I called in a doctor, who said that her chest was weak and Glasgow not the place for her in winter. She reluctantly agreed to go to her married sister in Wales – both her parents were dead – during the worst months in Glasgow. On January third, at the Central Station, we parted, she in tears, I, in my selfishness, with a sense of relief.

As the weeks passed I found it very difficult to resist her pleadings to come back to the studio; but for the doctor's warning me of the danger to her life I should have risked everything in my desire, even the royal picture. Fortunately for both of us the rush of sitters filled up my every moment, three and sometimes four a day coming to the studio, broken at intervals by my having to go out to them. I had no assistance, no secretary or anyone to help me make and keep appointments scattered all over England, Ireland, Scotland, and Germany. Still the memory of that cold, bleak morning on the platform of the Central Station could not be blacked out. The more exhausted I became with overwork the weaker my resolve not to see her again. It was little wonder that the strain was beginning to show itself, and without my knowing it the doctor was told to keep an eye on me. All that I can remember was that for some reason I believed in my sleep that I was being blackmailed for something terrible I had done, the nature of which I cannot remember. In the mornings I would leave my lodgings for the studio, believing that I should find in the letter box a sealed document denouncing me. The sense of terror as I reached the door was indescribable, as was the relief when I found nothing of an incriminating nature in my correspondence. As the day wore on and I got buried in my work I would gradually wake up to the fact that I had been dreaming and the whole thing was a nightmare that persisted in holding me in its clutches even when I was awake.

This had been going on slowly but surely getting worse until one morning early in March I found Kathleen in the studio. There she was in white muslin, the cheap stiff kind that was all that she could afford, seated on the model's throne, a vision of innocent loveliness, waiting in fear that I might be angry and send her back. She said nothing. I was beaten. Joseph Crawhall and Patrick Whyte came in and acted as witnesses while I went through the formula, "I, John Lavery, take you, Kathleen MacDermott, as my wedded wife," and so we were married. We were all sworn to secrecy until the completion of the royal picture. She was nineteen when Eileen was born, but she never recovered from it. Acute phthisis set in and within a year Kathleen passed away.

Whyte, who had nursed her through all her illness, taking her from one health resort to another, had finally rented a furnished villa at Kilmalcolm near Glasgow, where I could go daily. There was a little sheltered garden where Kathleen, all wrapped up, would sit in the sun when there was any and where Whyte, day after day, week after week, sat with her. I could only spare the week ends. There was a United Presbyterian Kirk near that made the Sundays hideous by the harsh clanging of a bell morning and evening. The days were shortening and growing too cold to sit out, and her cough was persistent. One Sunday morning the clanging bell was beginning. The nurse knocked at the door and said with characteristic Scottish brevity, "She is going." I heard Whyte on the stair saying in a strained voice, "Come quickly." She was being held up, breathing with difficulty, her large eyes staring straight out. I took the nurse's place, but her eyes did not move, though her lips smiled. I tried to whisper a prayer in her ear. I could just hear "Good-bye," a gasp, and her head fell forward. High up on the banks of the Clyde overlooking the Kyles of Bute she lies, under a simple headstone designed by Whyte.

Whyte now gave up his time and means to my child, calling himself the "nursery governor." There were two things he lived for: Eileen and the painting of his masterpiece, the "Ca' d'Oro" in Venice. He took a house in the country and lived with Eileen and her nurse through her babyhood, I with my head in a paintbox in London — forgetful. Eventually they came to live with me. The "Ca' d'Oro" and Eileen were inseparable; everywhere he went he talked of them. At the Chelsea Arts Club, where he was nicknamed "Permanent Whyte," the usual salutation was, "Hello, Whyte, how's Eileen, and how's the Ca' d'Oro?"

I had first met William Patrick Whyte — it annoyed him if it was spelt White — at l'Atelier Julien. He was the finest man I have known. He had rather a military appearance and was proud of some months spent as a volunteer in the Argyll and Sutherland Highlanders. He had been in an architect's office in Glasgow when his parents died, leaving him a couple of thousand a year. Then he decided to throw over architecture and study painting in Paris. He took a charming apartment on the Quai Bourbon and allowed me the use of one of his rooms as a studio. He would appear at Julien's regularly every morning about eleven o'clock, leisurely set up his easel and drawing carton, look at the model, sharpen his charcoal, have another look, make a few scratches, then spend some time in further contemplation, roll a cigarette, and look at some other fellow's work. Someone would call out "*L'heure model,*" and we would leave Whyte putting away his things for the morrow. And so day after day for weeks, when he would disappear for the rest of the term. He used to say, when people looked at his work, that everything they saw good in it they annexed as their own and all the bad they gave him credit for having done.

He spent his winters in Venice painting the Ca' d'Oro on the Grand Canal, going year after year, making many studies for it under different aspects of light until at last he found what he wanted. Then he got a 60″ x 40″ canvas and started on what was to be his masterpiece. For twenty years he worked at it, cutting a few inches off one side of it, adding to the other, taking it back each year, never completing it. He had frames cut to fit the varying shapes, having them cut or added to, the canvas becoming so loaded with paint and relinings that its weight was ten times more than that of the original picture. He would never let me touch it, though I assured him I could complete it in a day. He got rather sensitive about it. Once a friend said, "Whyte, if it is not a rude question, how long have you been working on the Ca' d'Oro?" "Well now," said Whyte, "suppose we discuss the question of rudeness first."

He was an honorable gentleman, — one of the few I have ever met, — with which he combined the wit of a genius. I cannot recall the brilliant gems he let fall (in days before men treasured up every bon mot so that it might be published and paid for). Three only I remember, and those three I lay here as a wreath on his memory. On religion: he said he did not attend church because prayer showed a want of confidence in the Creator. On morality: "I have never gone back on the devil for the pleasure he has given me." And when his income became considerably reduced he said: "I am living on the explanations of how my friends lost my money."

Perhaps the most noble and unselfish incident in his whole life was when he sacrificed himself that Kathleen might marry me. He was in love with her and she with him, but he had got it into his head that he would never arrive anywhere, and that she was far too beautiful to be tied to a failure. So he told her that I possessed every virtue and continued pleading for me until she consented to marry me.

VI

ROME AND GERMANY

I SPEAK of Rome fifty years ago, where I went after Kathleen's death. It seemed to me then both primitive and poverty-stricken. I was dazzled, of course, by the magnificent architecture — our Saint Paul's was a little miniature Saint Peter's — and the feeling that if Park Lane were built on the same scale as the Palazzo Venezia, the houses would have to be a thousand feet high. But I always seemed to be surrounded by beggars. Nor were the beggars the only poor. The poverty-stricken nobility made an effort to hide their case by driving about in hired coaches for an hour on the Corso and then going back to the chill of their icy *palazzi* to sit in freezing state and receive British and American tourists traveling under the auspices of Cook. No one without a title but all without a penny, and on the lookout for those in the reverse position, ready for a mutually advantageous exchange.

The churches still held a curious atmosphere of pagan Rome, and though the Madonna had taken the place of Venus the apostles looked much more like centurions. In the Pantheon I attended a requiem for Victor Emmanuel in semidarkness, the only light coming from the torches held by over a hundred cuirassiers, the light glittering on their breastplates and helmets, the place filling with smoke which slowly escaped through the hole in the roof. The rattle of the rifles at the word of command and the whole atmosphere of the scene made it difficult to realize that Christian worship was going on.

With the object of acquiring Italian I boarded with an impoverished noble family in a palace. It was sad and rather irritating to see the makeshifts they were put to in order to keep up appearances. Suffering from cold and hunger, they tried to hide it by feigning indifference and talking about their exalted position, while I knew that the whole source of their income came from two other boarders and myself. It was too depressing, and although I was truly sorry for them, one month was all I could stand; so I bade them farewell and found a magnificent studio of vast dimensions owned by a baron at that time in prison for financial fraud. It was so large that I often rode my bicycle about in it for exercise.

Although the furniture was scanty the walls were rich in tapestry painted in size-color. It is remarkable what the ordinary Italian house painter can do in the way of imitating materials and objects such as mantelpieces, skirting boards, and cornices. To get a room done in plain color with a whitewashed ceiling was said to be more expensive than a sky with clouds and tapestried walls. I asked why, and was told that it was more difficult to hide defects in the plaster when a plain wash was wanted. The real truth, I suspect, is that every Italian house painter is a scenic artist. The furniture was made as if for the stage, to be seen only from the front; all gold and glitter facing you, and the back not even planed or painted. It was a bit of a shock for me, coming from Scotland, where a piece of furniture can be seen with equal interest from all sides and where, no doubt, our decorative sense is lost in the practical and a chair need not always have its back to the wall.

For some reason I was very unhappy in Rome and could not work – hence these few depressing notes. But in the Sabine Hills, just outside the city, there is a little village which claimed my fancy tremendously and remains very clearly in my memory. Called Anticoli, it is built well on the side of the hill, so that its streets are stairways. That was the first thing about that village – you never walked through it, you climbed up it. And the second thing was that no one used money. All exchange was done by barter. There was one general store that supplied everything, from a needle to farm instruments. We saw eggs being exchanged for a rasher of bacon, the hire of a secondhand plough for a crate of chickens, and flour for sugar, pepper, and salt. I saw half a hundredweight of grapes turned down as of no value in exchange for macaroni. This was pitiful to see, but the people seemed to take it all as their just share in the scheme of things.

Many of the Roman artists' models came from this village. An artist of my acquaintance took me there one day. It was during a wine festival. The wine went to his head and he attempted to embrace a village girl called

Giovenella. She roughly pushed him away, and, drawing her knife, – used for pruning vines and an ugly weapon in a fight, – told him that her body was sacred. This sobered him up and, apologizing, he offered her marriage. But she refused, saying that their social positions prevented such an alliance – he was a lord and she was a peasant. They made up the quarrel and exchanged knives. Some years later, with extreme naïveté, he told me how he had met her again, and seeing her now married and fat and with three children, he had felt his romance shattered. What did he expect? She had even sold his knife for a lira. But the incident was of interest to me in showing the difference in outlook between the French and Italian models.

Before leaving Rome I had a letter from a German artist in London, Neven du Mont, telling me that a relative of his in Cologne would like me to go there to paint his wife. Thinking of Eau de Cologne, I addressed my letter "Herr von Guillaume, Cologne, France." However, it reached Köln all right, where, in spite of my geographical ignorance, I was received as a great artist.

The change from Rome made me feel I was now among my own people. In fact, like Lord Haldane, I found my spiritual home in Germany, where everyone I met spoke English and knew more about England and her customs than I could lay claim to. The Von Guillaumes, not satisfied with having me paint themselves and their relations, spread my fame far and wide. For five years I was overwhelmed with commissions up to the day when the Kaiser sent his unfortunate telegram to "Oom Paul," since when my work has not been in such great demand in Germany.

My first aerial flight was from Berlin to Posen in Poland. In those days all German balloons were military, under the command of a Prussian officer. Before getting permission to ascend I had to become an honorary member of the Luftschiffahrt Battalion. Our commander was a charming young man in Garde du Corps uniform, Lieutenant Herwarth von Bittenveldt. No one could have been more astonished than I to hear him ordering around, as if they were dogs, the Polish peasants who helped us to assemble the deflated balloon and carry it to the nearest station. I showed my astonishment, and the *Kleiner Leutnant* said they were canaille of the lowest order and had to be treated as such or we would have been attacked by them. I must say I saw anything but aggressiveness on their part – rather the opposite.

The five years I spent in Germany were perhaps the most agreeable since my student days in Paris. The hospitality was unbounded, most of my sitters were non-Aryan and most understanding – as a rule more so than Aryans. One afternoon, in the Unter den Linden, I was with Neven du Mont, who introduced me to Mary Auras, the niece of a well-known painter. She was then sixteen and gave me the inspiration for "Spring," now in the Luxembourg, and also for many other pictures –

"Mary in Green," "Mary in Black," "Mary with Roses," "The Green Coat," and numerous others, mostly in public galleries at home and abroad.

When Mary came to London she was a companion for my daughter. She knew but little English then, and her first attempts to manage it were often very amusing. One day, in my studio, she met a very lovesick young man who had just been jilted. Her sympathy for his despair led her to remember the following verse from Heine: —

Teurer Freund, Du bist verliebt,
Und dich qualen neue Schmerzen,
Und ich seh' des Herzen Glut
Schon durch deine Weste brennen.

And this, with the aid of a dictionary, she translated as follows: —

My dear Friend, I think you are in love,
And you have so many pains,
I see the heart-fire burning
Through your blooming waistcoat.[1]

One day I had finished the portrait of a lady in very décolleté dress; criticizing this picture, Mary remarked, "The color of the meat (*Fleischfarbe*) is very good." I wish I could remember her many translations from German, but I must say that it was not long before her English was much better than my German, in spite of the five winters I had spent in Berlin.

[1] Flowered waistcoats were the fashion in those days.

Some years later I decided to revisit Morocco and pass a winter in my villa at Tangier. My daughter and Mary accompanied me, and little did I dream that the latter was destined to remain in that country. Often attending the local sport of pigsticking and polo, she made the acquaintance of one Nigel d'Albini Black-Hawkins, who, after serving in South Africa with the Mounted Infantry during the Boer War, had settled down in North Africa. Before my return to England Mary and Nigel were married in the cathedral in Gibraltar. So Mary remained in Morocco, where she has taken a keen and useful interest in Moorish art, and in later years has given several private exhibitions of leatherwork specially designed for her by native craftsmen.

In the Schultz Gallery in Berlin the Emperor and Empress came to see my pictures, and, not knowing that Mary was German, expressed their belief that no such type of beauty existed in Germany as was depicted in "Spring" and the other pictures of her. When I first saw the Emperor, his quick movements and energetic manner reminded me of Theodore Roosevelt. His Majesty expressed pleasure in my work and said to the Empress how greatly he was disappointed that so little attention was paid when he told German artists what they should do. He spoke favorably of Adolf Menzel, and Lenbach, and even Liebermann's early work gained his approval, but he found Corinth, Slovaght, Franz Stück, and others of their school coarse.

I was invited to Mecklenburg-Schwerin to paint a portrait of the Duchess. She was a bit of an artist herself, with ideas that, added to the exigencies of a small German court, delayed progress. She was a charming lady, but such are the effects of art on some people that we were having little differences that came to a head with, "When Sartoris was in my father's service" (her father being King of Saxony). Not realizing that he was a court painter I quite innocently remarked, "Was that before he became an artist?" The fat was in the fire. Feeling that I might consider the incident closed I packed up, taking the picture with me, and was quite surprised two months later to receive a personal letter from Her Highness hoping that they would soon have the portrait. I apologized for the delay and sent it off in the state in which she had last seen it, expecting an explosion. Instead I got a most kind letter of appreciation.

She died the following year, and a little packet with a letter arrived from her husband stating that she had expressed a desire that I should receive one of her paintbrushes as a souvenir.

VII

JOSEPH CRAWHALL AND THE GLASGOW SCHOOL

CRAWHALL was the artist to whom the Glasgow School owed its greatest distinction. No artist I have known could say more with fewer brush strokes. In appearance – except for his eyes, which were a very deep brown and unusually intelligent – he might have been taken for a whipper-in. He had a long sallow face like that of a North American Indian, and rarely spoke unless he had something to say. Graham nicknamed him "the Great Silence," but he had acute observation and a ready wit on occasion. Usually, however, his pencil was to him what the tongue is to other men.

When he first came to Glasgow he signed himself "Jos. Crawhall, Jnr." and did so as long as his father was alive. The latter was a Yorkshire country squire and a close friend of Charles Keene, whom he supplied with many rough drawings astonishing in their significant simplicity, illustrating humorous scenes which Keene turned in a remarkable way into perfect little masterpieces for *Punch*. Crawhall's only real teaching came from his father, who insisted on his drawing from memory exclusively and would never permit any corrections to be made. He did get to Paris for a short time to the studio of Aimé Morot, whose teaching was entirely at variance with his early training. When drawing from life he was quite unable to eliminate irrelevant facts, which he found it so easy to do when drawing from memory. He practically never drew from nature and never used a sketchbook, but he would spend days or even weeks observing, and no essential detail or color was ever missed; he seemed to take a mental photograph of everything he wanted to know, and could develop and paint it at any time afterwards. At the time the critics pointed out that he must have been strongly influenced by Japan, but actually he never saw a Japanese print until he was twenty. He stood before it for a long time in silence, and then with the greatest enthusiasm wished to buy it.

He had his first one-man show in 1894, in Alex Reid's galleries in Glasgow, and his only other at Paterson's in London. The greater number of the pictures were at once bought by such Scottish collectors as Sir William Burrell and Mr. A. Coates. I think he showed once at the Royal Academy, and when we started the International Society he was on the Council and always exhibited. In 1909 he joined the New English Art Club, but his irregular habits of work and the persistence with which he destroyed his drawings made his output extremely limited. The critics were always enthusiastic. I remember Mr. Frank Rinder in the *Art Journal* saying:

"His 'Black Rabbit' may well be the nineteenth-century equivalent of Dürer's wonderful 'Hare.'"

After he left Glasgow, Crawhall bought a house in Yorkshire where he lived with his mother and sister, but he mixed very little with the neighboring families. Nevertheless they appreciated his work highly and used to circulate among themselves the very few pictures he allowed to pass his rigorous self-censorship, each keeping a picture for a few months at a time. My daughter Eileen used to spend her school holidays there. He never allowed anyone to watch him work, but he made an exception in her case, and the two became inseparable friends. He made endless sketches for her on the pages of an old washing book which fortunately she valued sufficiently to make into a scrapbook. But for each drawing he made to amuse a child half a dozen must have been thrown away because they did not come up to the high standard he set himself. Yet everything he did seemed to possess the value of a certain permanence – even his decorations of a notice left on the studio door by a friend, or the envelope of a letter to Eileen.

Whistler did not care much for his work, but I think I learned more from Crawhall than I did from the American master. Had I realized this fifty years ago I might have profited. The critic excuses the extraordinary productions of the painter or sculptor of to-day on the grounds that they see from the inside and are therefore incomprehensible to the general public, who see only from the outside and sometimes not even that. Crawhall's art includes all the dimensions I want to see. It is sad to think that he was cut off while still young, and destroyed much more of his work than he ever allowed to reach the public eye.

This wonderful economy of line Crawhall had in common with Phil May, and in appearance these great artists might have been twins, they were so alike. The similarity extended even to their mode of life, except that May married and Crawhall remained single. Phil was the more extreme in dress, and the last time we met he came to his studio door wearing the loudest suit I had ever seen. Seeing my look of surprise, he smiled and said, "Come in and listen to it, dear boy." Crawhall showed little interest in the work of other painters. I remember one day in the New Gallery calling his attention to a picture painted on silk by Conder. All he said was, "Umph. Whiskey and Watteau."

To-day he still remains little known to the general public, although an excellent selection of his pictures was shown both at Glasgow, in 1934, and at the recent exhibition of Scottish Art at Burlington House. In a few lines he could sketch an animal, making it more recognizable than the most candid camera could do — and this from memory. If he did a pack of hounds the huntsman would be able to recognize every single one, even when it was only indicated in half a dozen marks on the linen or paper he happened to be working on. In his oils there was never a false note in tone or color, and of course the drawing was beyond reproach. Oddly enough, I used to compare him with John Roberts, the billiards champion, in that they both eliminated every difficulty in their work. They were the two greatest masters I have ever known.

Although Joseph Crawhall's art thrilled me more than that of James Guthrie, it was the latter's personality and intellectual power that captured me completely. No painter I have known had a clearer conception of art, as may be gathered from the following letter: —

MY DEAR JOHN, —

You ask me about Matisse etc. Really I don't know the work of these men very well. But if it had attracted me I should have known it, you may be sure, much better than I do. It had never seemed worth following up; at the best sectional, the development of certain qualities at too great a cost, at the worst merely sensational. By this last I do not mean that those who produced it did so consciously only to attract notice at any price, but that it appeals too much to sensation pure and simple and is shallow.

I cannot think that the great stream is now represented by these French rivulets. Had I thought so when we were young I should have paused before giving up my life to art — there would not have been sufficient interest by a long chalk.

By all means let us keep our minds and eyes open, but let us not be weak enough to scrap all our canons to join painters and press-men who are so afraid of being thought reactionary and *démodé* that they seem to have lost all sense of scale.

To me, nothing that forces one or perhaps two elements in Art, to the exclusion of others, is great. It may compel attention, but it won't wash in the long run. It is good for youth to be extreme within reason, but the hurry-scurry and cocktail habits of modern life have no place in the Art region. Some seem to have dealt so much in *apéritifs* and sauces that the healthy appetite for the real food of the spirit has gone.

But you will say that I am old and out of it! I am glad to be out of that sort of thing and am too much interested in painting to have time to follow the *dernier cri.*

Yours ever,
JAMES GUTHRIE

From the day we met, in 1882, until the day of his death we were the closest companions. He was sensitive to the critics and tried not to show it; but once he broke. It was his first and only one-man show in London; he was given the smaller of two rooms at Doudswell's for the finest group of pastels I have seen, and in the larger gallery was another collection of the most meretricious but popular oils. It was a private view, and hundreds came to view the oils but only half a dozen came to see the pastels, I among them. When we were alone tears came into his eyes. That and what the Royal Academy stood for cured him of his desire to live in London.

No artist could have taken greater pains, not even Whistler, to make his work complete; often years would elapse between the beginning and the end of a portrait.

Sir Abe Bailey gave three commissions for three large portrait groups: "The Sailors," "The Soldiers," and "The Statesmen" who won the War, by Cope, Sargent, and Guthrie – now in the National Portrait Gallery. After working five years and completing his portrait on an oblong canvas like the others, it occurred to Guthrie that if three similar canvases were placed in a row, monotony would result; so, after serious consideration, he got a new canvas, changed the composition to an upright design, and spent five more years upon it. The critics were not at all kind and with a few exceptions failed to grasp the greatness of the work. This last blow hastened the end.

Besides Crawhall and Guthrie there were the others: Macgregor, Walton, Henry, Roche, Kennedy, Paterson, Melville, and Macaulay as the prophet of our Glasgow School. Harrington Mann, the master painter of children, let me have his studio, which at that time was the best in Glasgow, while he went to study under Legros at the Slade. We had a following of younger men: Gould, Park, MacAdam, Frew, Spence, Pirie, and others. This Glasgow School has scattered, but I hope that one day Macaulay will write its history, for there is no one alive who could do it so well. It was largely owing to his enthusiasm that we were held together. He founded and edited the *Scottish Art Review* to promote art criticism by artists, and to enlighten the public. If we all had had the singleness of mind, not to mention the literary talent, of the Editor, I feel certain it would have had a long life. His slogan was "Progress and Poverty." We were all for Progress, but Poverty did us in. My own share in the venture was putting my name to an article he wrote on Mary Queen of Scots. He left no stone unturned to keep the journal alive, but it came to a premature end after the first year. In 1903 I remember his writing enthusiastically: –

There's a future in landscape art. It is just in its infancy – born yesterday. I see it. I won't live to do it – but I'll try to get a little bit on the way. It will be done, and when it is done the result will be fit to go alongside the Elgin Marbles and Whistler's portrait of his mother. I have no doubt whatever that the people of Scotland (I don't mean the populace), my countrymen – those who peg away at this thing because of the imperious urge within them – will in the course of the next few generations say the big thing in landscape, do with it what Beethoven and Wagner did with music, take it and shape it anew to larger and finer issues. I'm as certain of this as that I breathe – in fact, I see it as a plain fact and can prove it up to the hilt to any intelligent mind. That's why I wouldn't go away from Scotland if I got a million a year. Heavens, how my heart swells and squirms within me when I *see* my ain countree. . . . John, landscape art will yet write the Bible of this revelation for the common people and they will hear the Gospel gladly. Not all the people – but those who are ripe for it.

You think it is a survival in me of the old notions – mistaken enthusiasm, John – but it is a deeper and deepening conviction with me, it is the very breath of life for me.

But not only was he our prophet, he was also our critic – and a rigorous one. I remember when I was painting the "Night after the Battle of Langside," which up till then had been my biggest effort. It had cost me two years of continuous work, and I proposed to take London by storm with it at the Royal Academy. As the sending-in day drew near Macaulay grew anxious. I had intended sending it the previous year but he had stopped me, saying that it was the soul of Scotland but it was unfinished. I was determined that this should not happen again, and I had it packed and arranged to travel with it, in spite of his strong opposition. He was so determined that I should not show it that he kept arguing to the very last minute, and as the train was moving out of the station he jumped into my third-class smoker – which in those days meant sitting on wooden benches. He continued his arguments all night until we reached St. Pancras more dead than alive, he with talking and I with listening. He won. The picture went back to Glasgow with the case unopened.

Shortly after I had decided to stay in Glasgow the Grosvenor Gallery was organized by Sir Coutts Lindsay, in support of the Pre-Raphaelites and others whose work was not in favor at the Royal Academy. We Glasgow men were given a show that opened up Germany, Austria, and Belgium, and later France, Italy, and Spain. There we found much appreciation and encouragement, our pictures being bought for the various national and municipal collections on the Continent.

For some years I had been submitting my pictures to the Selection Committee of the Royal Academy without gaining admission. The situation was getting serious, especially for a portrait painter, because the public had so much faith in the Academy that an artist whose work was rejected was accounted second-rate or worse. Nowadays things have changed, and an artist is said to be second-rate if he *is* a member of that body! On the last occasion, when I received a note regretting that a place could not be found for me, I decided to wait until I was invited – which happened some ten or twelve years later.

VIII

CUNNINGHAME GRAHAM

It was at about this time that I first met Cunninghame Graham, who invited me to Gartmore, his ancestral home in the Rob Roy country. A grim old Spanish woman received us in the hall – there seemed to be no other servants. Yet there must have been some, for the house, though half denuded of furniture, was free from dust and scrupulously clean. I remarked on the strange look of some of the portraits. "Yes," he said, "an ancestor of mine had a local painter to paint over their faces with those of his cronies. He spent all the money he could get in lowering the house by raising the ground around it, thereby impoverishing the estate so much that I have nothing to live on. You see he had great taste but for the most part bad."

John Burns joined us on this occasion at Gartmore, for it was just at this time that they had both come out of Pentonville, where they had served six weeks' hard labor for their share in the Trafalgar Square riots over the question of free speech – the two of them taking on, so they claimed, single-handed, the constabulary numbering five thousand. I asked them about their experiences in prison. Hard labor they considered less irksome than ordinary imprisonment, for with the former you were given plenty of coarse food, and the time passed; while with the latter you were starved and left to pass the time in contemplation. There was a parson in the next cell to him, said Graham, who was in "for an old ecclesiastical failing." Burns was very proud of his biceps, which he exposed, and Graham equally so of his agility with the foils, which he demonstrated from time to time with the aid of his walking stick as we strolled in the cool of the evening.

Graham purchased from the tramway company a wild Argentine pony that refused to go into harness. He named him Pampa, and insisted on my painting a picture of himself in complete cowboy outfit on the pacing steed. Then I painted him frankly in the manner of Velásquez, full-length and life-size, a harmony in brown, which he christened "Don Roberto, Commander for the King of Aragon in the Two Sicilies." (The equestrian group he presented to Buenos Aires, and the "Commander" was purchased by the Corporation of Glasgow.) It was concerning the latter that Bernard Shaw said, "He is, I understand, a Spanish hidalgo, hence the superbity of his portrait by Lavery (Velásquez being no longer available). He is, I know, a Scotch laird. How he continues to be authentically the two things at the same time is no more intelligible to me than the fact that everything that has ever happened to him seems to have happened in Paraguay or Texas instead of Spain or Scotland."

When I knew him at this time his finances were in a shocking state and things were getting unbearable down at Gartmore. Suddenly he wrote to say that he could stand it no longer. Would I come down at once and see him end it all with Pampa in a spot where I had painted a view of the Rob Roy country that he loved?

I wired back, "Ill in bed wait till next week." Thus I postponed his death for forty years.

He was very fond of William Morris and often used to talk to me about him. He liked the incongruities and eccentricities of the man. He liked his habit of grinding his teeth openly on the platform while waiting for the train at Earl's Court, of throwing ill-cooked food out of the window, of weeping over a disappointment, of swearing like a trooper, of fidgeting like a child if forced to sit still, of permitting his great mane of hair and beard to bristle and his eyes to flame with actual fire if someone disagreed with him on Burne-Jones's art, of beating his head against the wall, of biting the furniture, of tearing his tapestries, of pulling down his curtains. It especially appealed to Graham that Morris not only made furniture but bit furniture, for it always rather worried him that this man who couldn't wear a tie yet made so many things that pleased the precious. He was delighted that Morris had once confessed to him, "I have spent, I know, a vast amount of time designing furniture and wallpapers, carpets and curtains; but after all I am inclined to think that that sort of thing is mostly rubbish, and I would prefer for my part to live with the plainest whitewashed walls and wooden chairs and tables." When Morris died Graham wrote a description of the funeral in the *Saturday Review.* It has often been referred to as a literary gem, and Bernard Shaw is reported to have said of it, "He'd wipe the floor with us all if he often wrote like that." Graham himself was not displeased with it and gave me a copy. I will quote a bit of it here in view of the fact that my literary friends, who say that they know it and know that it is splendid, nevertheless can offer no proof that they have ever read it: –

Not that he was forgotten by those for whom he lived; for in a little group, forlorn, disheveled, and their eyes grown dim with striving for the Revolution, stood his own faithful house carles from Hammersmith, and they too followed their master to the end – standing upon the platform as it were, upon the brink of some new country over which they saw, but knew they could not enter.

So dust to dust fell idly on my ears and in its stead a vision of the England which he dreamed of filled my mind. The little Church grew brighter, looking as it were filled with the spirit of a fuller faith embodied in an ampler ritual.

John Ball stood by the grave, with him a band of archers all in Lincoln green, birds twittered in the trees, and in the air the scent of apple-blossom and white hawthorn hung. All was much fairer than I had ever seen the country look, fair with a fairness that was never seen in England but by the poet, and yet a fairness with which he labored to endue it. Once more the mist descended and my sight grew dimmer; the England of the Fellowship was gone, John Ball had vanished and with him the archers, and in their places remained the knot of countrymen, plough-galled and bent with toil, the little Church turned grayer as if a reformation had passed over it. I looked again, the bluff bold kindly face had faded into the northwest wind.

Graham's financial affairs must have cleared up in some miraculous manner, for he was able to carry on as an amateur who did not have to make his living by pen or politics. (The truth was, he managed to sell Gartmore for £100,000.) Some people complain that he remained an amateur and playboy. But he was not an amateur in his own art, the art of personality. That art is rare and calls for great devotion and labor. It has few masters. As a portrait painter I have seldom found it. Graham's job was to create himself; he had the material. It was unnecessary for him to do more, like T. E. Lawrence (for whom he had great admiration, seeing in him a superb Irish playboy). But the latter had no personality – so he had to take Arabia.

I think I did something to help Graham in the creation of his masterpiece – himself. He was flattered and grateful (and did all he could to advertise the success of my first important one-man show, which I called "A Dream of Fair Women" and which was held at Lawrie's in Glasgow in 1890). And later he cracked up my powers of concentration in the following terms, which give me too much pleasure to be omitted. We were at Tangier together, and he wrote afterwards: –

I used to come upon him seated like a fly in amber in the little winding path which leads out to the Soko de Afuera, surrounded by a crowd. Moors stood and gazed, Jews chattered, and Spanish boys made those profane remarks which make them celebrated amongst the swearers of the world. Mules, laden with great trusses of pressed straw, brushed by his easel, and now and then a camel came sailing past, appeared about to take a piece out of his umbrella, as he sat buried in his work. All left him unconcerned, and it may be that in that passage in Tangier he learned the trick of working quite unconcerned by anything that passes in the world, which truly stands him in such stead in his own studio. This is the chiefest miracle about him, and it appears to me almost as wonderful as the recurring and continuous miracle of the flower and the leaf, the tides, day and night, and the mysterious rising of the stars, all of which we know are really simple things and follow natural laws, but at the same time pass our comprehension to declare, still less to demonstrate.

Cram me a studio full of ladies, all exhaling scent, dump me a crowd of foolish *flâneurs* in a corner, all babbling about Art, a journalist or two, art critics three or four, a picture dealer, one or two frame-makers, some Glasgow painters up for a week in town, a couple flirting in the dark, two or three children playing on the floor; and there at his Whistler table-palette, his back turned on to a mirror, and with his patient seated on the throne, Lavery still paints away. The person who is being painted chats with her friends; doors close and open; someone has just forgotten that she has left her husband sitting in a shop, and screeches down the telephone telling him not to be a fool; scents, noise, confusion, the strains of a man grinding out a piece on a pianola — all affect him just as little as the condition of the poor affects Parliament, as he sits painting on. He answers everyone with a smile, not in the least regarding what they say, but in proportion to their folly, and still the picture grows. Now he steps back, just missing treading on a lady's toes. She begs his pardon, and he, courteously smiling, accepts the excuse, just as he pardons and accepts all other follies that afflict the world and come between the painter and his work. Often when he has painted I have sat watching, and now and then obstructing to the best of my ability, with talk, with criticisms, or when I could not find the cigarettes. All has been useless, and before my eyes the picture (sometimes my own) has steadily advanced. All things to all men was good enough for the apostle to the North Britons; but to be all things to all women one must be Irish, and a portrait painter.

IX

MOROCCO

AFTER my success with "A Dream of Fair Women" I was for a time affluent enough to do some riding, including a hunt or two. I even rode in the Row. But that soon became exceedingly boring, its monotony and dullness enervating and exhausting. It is hard to understand the restless Cunninghame Graham enjoying it, as he did to the last, unless we remember that he had a personality to think about and keep building up.

However, this riding came in very handy, for after I had got to know Graham we decided to go to Morocco together, and to accept the guiding out there of Walter Harris, correspondent to *The Times,* who spoke every known Arabic dialect so fluently that he was able to pass himself off as a Moor – except when he failed in this on one occasion and was sentenced to death.

On arriving we found that Harris had arranged a trip for us into the interior with all the necessary impedimenta. It was a great opportunity for me and I was more than delighted at being allowed to join in. The first stop on a roadless journey was Arzila, a beautiful little white Moorish town on the coast on the way to Alcazar el Kebir. That was the first day, uneventful except for the pleasure and excitement of seeing new things. But at that time in Morocco you never knew what might happen next — as we found on the following day. In the early morning Walter Harris rode ahead, Graham next, I following in the rear. I saw them disappear over the brow of the hill, and when I reached the top, one of the most paintable pictures I have ever seen was before me. On a flat plateau were assembled some dozens of mounted warlike Moors. In the centre of the picture was Harris, gesticulating with the leader. On a further hillside a host of ferocious-looking fellows, riding two on every horse and mule, were fast approaching. I rode up to Harris and Graham, feeling that we were in for it by the way these men fingered their knives and drew forth their pistols. Were they going to shoot us or only dishorse us? And for what cause? But Harris was a man of great resource and continued an eloquent oration. At last there was a change in the tone of the chief, and Harris took out his notebook, wrote something, and passed it over. The chief examined it in a way that showed he had no notion of what was written, kissed the paper, touched his brow, shook hands, and allowed us to proceed.

Harris then told us that their village had been raided the night before and their cattle and young women carried off by a neighboring tribe. To retrieve them they would have to pass through land held by El Raisuli, the famous brigand. Walter had explained to them that he had authority from El Raisuli to pass his friends through without molestation. We asked if this were really true and he said that it was, to the extent of their being allowed to pass through; whether they would ever get back safely with their cattle was another question.

The country was lovely. It was February. Not the February we know in England, when everything is dead and nothing yet born. In steady sunshine our horses waded girth-deep through the amazing verdure of wild hyacinth, anemones, and narcissi stretching away to a ringed horizon.

And then the change. The entering into Alcazar that evening. The contrast from so much beauty to so much filth, from the fragrance of the flowers to the stench of excrement. The narrow streets were strewn with entrails and other fetid matter, with an occasional pool of blood where a sheep had been recently slaughtered. It had been raining and the horses slithered through the slime. Storks perched everywhere, gorging on the putrid mess. Women swathed in white, only their eyes showing, looking rather like surgeons at an operation, passed by on donkeys. But the poor were forced to wade on foot. Outside, a bank about fifty feet high and twenty broad surrounded the whole town. It was the accumulation of centuries of refuse which had become overgrown.

It was here that I first met Bibi Carleton. Some people feel that they have been born into the wrong sex, and wear the clothes and follow the behavior of the sex they favor. It also happens that some men feel that they have been born into the wrong century or the wrong race — and spend their lives trying to put that right. Bibi was an Englishman who felt that he should have been an Arab. He mixed with the people of Arabia better than with his own people. He spoke Arabic better than English. He was more at ease, he felt more natural, on a horse in the desert than in a car on the highroad. He chose the all-reeking streets of Tangier for his university. His swarthy face, his loud voice, his peculiarly un-English walk, removed him still further from the country of his birth.

I didn't see very much of him, but he was with us some of the time and occasionally did me the honor of playing pranks on me — one of which I shall presently mention.

I am anxious to recount only those things which will interest the reader as well as myself, so I will avoid the set description of a set journey, and will give a few isolated scenes that appeal to me still.

The Soko in the afternoon is a very different place from what it was in the morning, when the market is in full blast packed with a mass of shouting men and screaming women, mingled with the silvery tinkle of the bell of the water carrier and the many notes coming from donkey noise, horse noise, camel noise, sheep noise, and goat noise. Add to this the uplifted voices of the halt, the maimed, and the blind pleading for alms from the Christian, who, as a rule, is mounted and indifferent to everything but his own importance as he forces those on foot to make way. But in the afternoon the place is empty except for the snake charmer and his audience, and the storyteller and those who squat in a circle and listen with deep interest to his tales of love and adventure.

On one occasion Graham was much struck with their patience and silent appreciation, indicated by signs to each other when any absorbing incident was recounted. And as he gazed at this audience he fell to thinking of the House of Commons and his constituents and the Eight-Hour Day, which was a favorite topic of his just then. What progress he would make, he thought, if he had people like that to talk to! Carried away on the spur of the moment, he stepped forward and asked if he might say a few words on a subject he had much at heart. The Moors nodded their heads, and in his imperfect Arabic he began an impassioned address on the Eight-Hour Day. He had not got very far before he realized that his audience was not in the least sympathetic; in fact they were examining their flintlocks and feeling for their knives when a friendly Moor, seeing the situation, whispered in his ear, "These men have never worked *one* hour a day in their lives, and are prepared to wade through blood before they work eight."

One morning the rest of the party went off looking for bustards, I, with a paintbox, looking for a *motif.*

We arranged to meet at a certain place for lunch – one bottle of wine being reserved for each of us. Having struck an exciting subject, I worked long past the luncheon hour. When I discovered the time I quickly packed up and made a run for it. In my haste I kicked over a hornets' nest and ran for all I was worth with hornets in a cloud over me. I was tripped up by a tree stump and fell headlong into soft black mud, holding with both hands the brim of my panama down over my neck. I had to let go, feeling I was for it. I scrambled to my feet to see the hornets depart without leaving a single sting. I have often thought of my escape and wondered at it. Completely exhausted, and parched with thirst, I arrived at the place we had arranged for lunch. There were my three companions lying under the shade of a large olive tree basking in comfort, the remains of luncheon scattered around, including all the wine bottles completely empty. When they saw me they made signs, pointing to a large dark object in the branches of the tree where the horses were tethered. Before I could show my indignation and anger at their selfishness in drinking my share of the wine, Bibi, with a finger on his lips to enjoin silence, whispered, "Lavery, there's an eagle; take my gun and have a shot. Be careful of the ponies." I had remarked that morning that it would give me pleasure to bring down an eagle, so forgetting my thirst for a moment I took the gun and aimed at what turned out to be an eagle sure enough, but it was on its back with its talons in the air. They had shot it and planted it there. If I had been further from them I verily believe I should have given them a taste of the buckshot.

The further we got into the interior the greater became the evidence of the terrible state of the people. At the entrance to every village we came on half its inhabitants, and a sight they were, almost naked, in the last stages of starvation, many too weak to stand up. Old men, women, children, would hold out their hands and call attention in the name of Allah. I did not understand the manner in which they received alms, often with a look of rage rather than gratitude, until I was told their point of view, which was that we all come into the world bringing nothing; if you have riches and they have poverty you hold their share, and when you hand over a little of it you ought to be grateful and thank God that you have been given the opportunity of restoring what can only be ill-gotten. The young men, who would rather die than ask help of a Nazarene, hid themselves. I had seen photographs of the ravages of famine in India and isolated examples of what starvation meant at home, but nothing ever conveyed the horror of these scenes, intensified as they were by the insane waste and heartless cruelty of those in power from the Sultan downwards. We bought bread and went on our way feeling that we were different. Of course we were different; Christians do not tolerate such a state of affairs.

However, they are great stoics. I remember one day,

when a fight was going on between the Angera and Raisuli's men within sight of Tangier, Bibi and I rode as near as we dared to the seat of action. We saw a Moor in the distance with a human head stuck on the end of his rifle; when we got near he rolled off his horse. We galloped up; he was gasping for water, which we gave him. When he revived he showed us a gaping wound in his hip and asked for a cigarette, while Bibi with a jack-knife began probing it and extracted a good-sized bullet. Then, taking the paper off a couple of cigarettes, he plugged the hole with tobacco. All the time the Moor was lying back casually smoking and showing no sign of pain. But the one unbearable cruelty that can be inflicted on a Moor is solitary confinement. When the Moorish War Minister was sent with presents from the Sultan to King Edward VII on his Coronation, Kaid Maclean, who came with him as interpreter, begged that our prisons should not be shown. The Moorish prison in Tangier is a kind of show place in which visitors are allowed to look through a hole in the door into an open courtyard where poor wretches are chained up like dogs in a kennel. There is no kind of sanitary arrangement, nor are there food and drink other than what their friends bring in, but they are allowed to work at baskets, mats, and so on. Eyes are put out, hands are cut off, and other tortures are inflicted, and the Moor will face any of them saying that it is the will of God, but solitary confinement drives him raving mad in no time.

Owing to these conditions, the Sultan, fearing an inconvenient discontent amongst the people, at Kaid Maclean's suggestion decided for the sake of appearances to set up a newspaper printed in Fez. So an up-to-date press was sent from England and, as the Sultan could not wait a minute, it was set up in the open on his tennis court and a paper printed at once. By the second edition he lost interest. The press stood about five feet high on the lawn when we first saw it. On my next visit some years later it was still standing on the lawn, but had practically sunk beneath the ground, being overgrown by the vegetation. With the rains it was gradually disappearing. I may add that the Sultan was not in the least perturbed by this any more than by the fate of his grand piano, which, on its way to the palace, had fallen into a river and been carried down to the sea. When it was eventually brought to the surface it was found that the top had fallen open, and so many fish had caught in the chords that they decided to drop it in again.

My first sight of a Moorish girl's face was after dinner in the house of a rich Moor in Fez. Four dancing girls came in and disported themselves one at a time in what is known as a *danse du ventre*, in a small circle formed by half a dozen men sitting crosslegged on mattresses. The first three were fat and ample, the fourth slim and snake-like, and at the end each lay stretched on her back with her head on the lap of the man of her choice, who was expected to place as many dollars on her head as he thought her worth. I, anxious to get the lithe lady to sit, placed what an American would call "my bottom dollar," but she refused. Walter, seeing my disappointment, said, "I'll get a couple to come to our tents to-morrow morning." In the morning, at 6 A.M., two shapeless bundles in white were ushered in to me. When they unveiled they exposed the bedaubed, grinning faces of two of the most hideous beldams I have ever seen out of a brothel — where they had really come from. What an opportunity for a surrealist!

Some time after, I was invited to dine with the Basha of Tetuan, who allowed female slaves to serve unveiled. Walter, knowing my interest, advised me to be careful and on no account pay any attention to them, telling me that some years ago this same Basha was entertaining Christians, and a young subaltern from the garrison at Gibraltar remarked to his host on the beauty of one of the girls. Next morning he was presented with a box neatly done up in which he found her head.

Walter made up for this later by introducing me to Kaid Maclean, who charmed the Sultan by the skirl of his bagpipes so successfully that he became a favorite at the palace. We were entertained by his family, and Nora, his eldest daughter, made it possible for me to get a view of the interior of a harem from a distance and from a point where I could not be seen. I spent a week in a very uncomfortable and cramped position painting the picture. Most of the time the place was empty, and at no time did I see the women do anything other than lie about talking, singing, playing the *gimbri,* and behaving in the orthodox manner in which I had been told they spent their lives. They were not more than fifty feet from where I was hidden, a deep pool dividing us, and only fear of getting the Kaid and his daughters into difficulties prevented me from getting a "close-up" when the picture was completed. Not that there was anything fascinating about the ladies, but I was intrigued to know where the clocks were. At least a dozen kept striking with tinkling chimes quite independent of each other and the hours recorded. They were out of sight and almost drove me crazy.

Years later, still on the hunt for Eastern beauty, I was the guest of Rudolph d'Erlanger in his Arab palace at Sidi-bu-Saïd in Tunis. I told him how much I should like to paint an Arab lady, for up to that time I had never seen one. The Master of his Household said he thought it could be arranged. The Bey of Tunis was on an expedition and not likely to return for weeks. The chief eunuch in charge of the harem was known to my friend, who thought that a nice present would go a long way with him. It was generally known that one girl in the harem was the most beautiful in all Tunisia and he was sure that things could be arranged. It was all settled, and she came, a fat, hideous woman dressed with fantastic splendor. For a moment I could not think how to get out of it, so proposed that as the Bey would be away and the only canvas I had was too small for such magnificence, there would be time to telegraph to Paris for a much larger one, and to show her how quickly I could work I proceeded to paint a slave with a black baby that was standing by, and so got out of a cul-de-sac.

Years afterwards, when I recalled that scene, I saw what I had missed – a real Oriental instead of the artificial thing I was searching for. Blinded by what I wanted, I could not see how wonderful a picture I might have painted of the Pride of the Harem. Unfortunately that was not the only time I had missed an opportunity of recording a side of Moorish life that would have been of interest – as in the case of the two ladies from the brothel mentioned above.

The greatest hindrance to my painting in Morocco was the natives' belief in the Evil Eye. I found this very difficult to overcome. All my Moorish sitters believed I possessed it and, no matter what their morals might be, jibbed against being painted. They were certain it meant being damned. I have come across Christians who shared the belief, thinking it might hasten the end.

A final memory of this journey I have kept to the last. One evening I was at Maclean's hotel, a largish place in the Soko, where about twenty cosmopolitans at a long table in a noisy jumble of languages were busy allaying their hunger and slaking their thirst. One rather dismal-looking stranger kept eyeing us, and when some of the others had left the table he edged up opposite and in an apologetic voice, with a strong Caledonian accent, said, "Beg pardon, gentlemen, but it is fine to hear one's own language spoken. Am just come this morning and there was a fine to-do on the boat, a daft man shooting everybody he could get at. If I had been sure of the scriptural acceptation of the situation I would have had a bang at him myself. Of course he might have plunked me, but I would have risked that. You see, I'm a missionary and I had the Word on me. I'm from Glasgow Cowcaddens District Mission, and no being very strong I was marked out for one of the foreign missions."

"Do you speak Arabic?"

"No."

"Then how do you intend to approach the Moor?"

"Well, as I told you, I carry the Word."

"That's all very well, but there is a Spanish Mission here and they have given up trying to convert the Moors; even the medical Mission, while accepted in illness, is discarded by them in health."

"Oh, ay, but they havena got the Word."

When I think of my times abroad with Cunninghame Graham and of the people I met while with him, it is this missionary armed with the "Word" and – to take a jump in space – the "Saint," a Spanish anarchist, that I remember most clearly.

The year of King Alfonso's wedding I returned to London from Tangier with Graham, and we stopped at Cádiz en route. The hall porter, who seemed to know Graham well, told him that a Communist friend of his had just been released from prison at Melilla, where he had served ten years in semidarkness and solitary confinement. Graham inquired where the "Saint" was to be found, and he was directed with much secrecy to the Anarchist Club, through a number of back streets into a dark, narrow lane. Some distance down, we saw a stream of bright light crossing the street and striking the white wall opposite, making the surrounding darkness more intense. When we got to it we saw it came from a doorway where a barber with a gleaming razor was at work. Graham had a whispered talk with him, and we were conducted down a long dark passage into a low-ceilinged room filled with tobacco smoke where sat a bearded crew of men who looked capable of anything. They all rose to their feet as we entered, but one came forward and shook hands with Graham. He was tall and very thin, with a cadaverous face and dark glasses, his thin lips showing the gums unpleasantly as he spoke. Before his imprisonment he had been the editor of an anarchist journal in London, so he spoke perfect English, but now he was scraping a living as a wine merchant's agent. Partly to show that I was at ease and partly in sympathy for his plight, I gave him an order for some dozen brandy. Afterwards I discovered that I was his first customer.

I told him that I was on my way to paint the wedding of King Alfonso; he was much interested and in the most matter-of-fact manner said, "If I were you I would not hurry to Madrid – there may be no wedding." There was something sinister about his mouth as he said this – I could not see his eyes – that gave me a feeling that I had got into bad company. I was sure of this a few days later when the bombs were thrown in the Puerto del Sol which came near to emptying the Spanish throne. For weeks afterwards, if anyone touched me or came up behind me suddenly, I would almost jump out of my skin.

X

WHISTLER AND THE INTERNATIONAL SOCIETY

FRANCIS HOWARD, a young man of considerable initiative and, like Whistler, of American extraction, was introduced to me as having a grand scheme whereby "outsiders" – that is, artists outside the Royal Academy – should form a society and include every artist of note in Europe and America. This appealed strongly to me at the time as I had just had the usual note from the Royal Academy asking me to remove my work, which had been rejected again. I jumped at Howard's scheme, and for ten long years turned my back on Burlington House and joined forces with Whistler and the others. We made out a long list of members qualifying for the International Society of Sculptors, Painters, and Gravers, and asked Whistler to be the first President. He consented and passed the list, complimenting us on our selection. There was one name that I had suggested to him before our list was made up – Walter Sickert. "What," he said, pretending to take something from his breast pocket, "my Walter, whom I put down for a minute and who ran off? Oh no, not Walter."

Although we at Glasgow worked with a richer palette

than Whistler, we recognized in him the greatest artist of the day and thought of his "Ten O'Clock Lecture" as the Gospel of Art. Yet none of us ever saw him at work or knew his procedure. I remember a friend of mine sitting to him every day for many weeks and telling me how exacting he was in not permitting him to move for an hour at a time. I was surprised when I saw this portrait to find no evidence of work other than might have been done in a couple of sittings. There was little paint and the canvas gave no evidence of having had the paint removed. I asked how he managed to hide the work he put in it. Adjusting his eyeglass he went up close to it, scrutinizing it very carefully, and said, "You see, my dear Lavery, that's how we do it."

Théodore Roussel told many stories of the studio — one in particular of how the *cher maître* proceeded with a portrait. He would first of all make a slight sketch in charcoal, then, after a very careful study, he would decide that there were so many different tones of flesh color, so many more for the clothes, background, and so forth. These he would mix and put into little pots, keeping the paint moist with water. It might take weeks before the day came when he would apply them to the canvas. No doubt this was one of his scientific experiments, to be discarded when it did not work.

One evening Théodore Roussel came to the Chelsea Arts Club in great excitement; he had got a commission from a rich patron. After he had been working at it for a month, telling us in the interval how it was progressing, at last he said it was finished. A few days afterwards I went to his studio, hoping to see it. When I asked where it was he pointed to about fifty little pots, saying, "*Le voilà!*"

I do not know whether it was because I was more respectful and said "Sir" and "Mr. Whistler" while others called him "Jimmy," but when he was elected President of the International Society I was made Vice President and Howard Honorary Secretary. Whistler always disliked familiarity. He said it was the "lowest form of intimacy." No sooner was he elected than he returned to Paris, having attended one or two council meetings, certainly not more than three. An absentee president did not make the inauguration of a new society any easier. He required the smallest details of its meetings to be reported to him at length, and rarely allowed time for this to be done adequately. He completely ignored the fact that almost daily letters were being sent reporting progress, and complained that he did not know what was going on.

We started by turning Prince's skating rink into a charming picture gallery, renting it from Admiral Maxse, an admirer of Mrs. Brown Potter, the actress, whose portrait by Mortimer Mempes he desired should have a prominent place in the first exhibition. Whistler got to hear of it and asked, "Who is Mempes?" – though he had known him well for years. He said he could not have bumboats like him on the quarter-deck. The Admiral answered in the same vein that he was not a bumboat, but a first-class frigate that would be a great addition to the Fleet. Besides, since he, the Admiral, had taken a share in the expenses, there was the financial side to be considered, and he thought that such an attractive subject would be a great draw. Whistler replied, "My dear Admiral, why not place your first-class frigate on rollers and run him round the rink in the season?"

Although the expenses were heavy we managed to make the first exhibition pay. The German artist, Auguste Neven du Mont, came to our aid in the second year by an anonymous gift of £500. Besides being an artist of considerable merit, he was Master of the East Sussex Foxhounds and a retired officer in the Uhlans. Whistler gained much publicity by having the comments of the press published in the catalogue, making the critics, as it were, eat their own words, and causing considerable amusement to the general public. He must have kept all printed criticisms, derogatory and otherwise, with this end in view. *The Times* critic had referred to the "vanished hand which drew the 'Symphony in White' and 'Miss Alexander.' " He quoted this view on the first showing of the picture, with the comment: "*Other Times, other lines.*" . . . The critic continued: "His portrait of Miss Alexander is certainly one of the strangest and most eccentric specimens of portraiture. . . . We should imagine he had merely made a sketch, and left it before the colors were dry, in a room where the chimney-sweeps were at work. . . . A child's portrait . . . uncompromisingly vulgar. . . . Before such portraits as the full-length portraits of Mr. Whistler, critic and spectator alike are puzzled! . . . After all, there are certain canons about what constitutes good drawing, good color, good painting, and when an artist deliberately sets out to ignore or violate all of these, it is desirable that his work should not be classed with that of ordinary artists."

We made some return in the ten years I occupied the chair for the recognition we had received on the Continent and in America. Up till our advent there was scarcely a modern foreign picture to be seen on exhibition in England except, perhaps, with dealers. It was considered unpatriotic to include the foreign artist, and we had a hard struggle because few were really interested in art outside their own country. "Nationalism is commonly held up to admiration as a high virtue," once said Lord Allenby, "while internationalism, which is, in other words, a generous sympathy for our fellow men, is branded as a crime, a surrender, a betrayal of our own particular interests and rights." At the first International Exhibition there was seen in London for the first time, so far as I know, the work of Degas, Manet, Forain, Monet, Cézanne, Renoir, Sisley, Toulouse-Lautrec, as well as many of the modern German, Italian, and Dutch painters who were unknown, even as names, to the general public.

From the beginning Whistler had insisted that to be a Member of the Royal Academy and of the International Society was incompatible. This caused trouble with artists who, while interested in the aims of the International, saw no reason to sever their allegiance to Burlington House. It came to a head when J. J. Shannon, having accepted the invitation to become a member of our committee, took no steps to resign from the Royal Academy. A year later Whistler was still writing on the subject as a matter of principle, and not from any personal animosity towards Shannon, of whom he always spoke with sympathy. It has been said that if Whistler had been offered membership in the Royal Academy he would have accepted it. I believe he would. He was an old friend of Sir Frederick Leighton – they were "Freddie" and "Jimmy" to each other – and when he was made President of the Society of British Artists (which he claimed to have made Royal) he received an invitation to a reception at the Royal Academy which he accepted. Leighton received his guests at the top of the stairs. There was a commotion when Whistler was observed ascending them. Leighton went forward with extended hand. "My dear Jimmy, this is the first time I have seen you here!" "Yes, Freddie," he replied in his most winning way. "It is quite true, and I have such a rotten excuse to offer you. *It is the first time I have been invited.*" When Whistler was outvoted as President of the Society of British Artists, he resigned with a number of adherents, saying, "The artists have come out, the British remain."

During this same spring of 1899 I approached Sargent with an invitation to become an Honorary Member, which he accepted, but on hearing of the trouble over Shannon's resignation from the Royal Academy he at once wrote: —

MY DEAR LAVERY, —

I hear there has been a complication with regard to Shannon, and that Whistler has decreed that he is to be deposed or something, because he is an Academician.

This puts a new light on our conversation of the other day, when I consented to your request to become an Honorary Member, and supposed your authority final. If I am in the position of being a Candidate for Honorary Membership proposed by you, but whose eligibility must be decided upon by a higher power, even God Almighty, I withdraw my name; for I am not soliciting the post and only consented on your saying it would be an advantage to the Society in the eyes of foreign contributors.

Please let me know exactly how the matter stands — whether I am already an Honorary Member, or whether that still remains to be decided.

Yours sincerely,
JOHN SARGENT

The next day I received another letter in which he amplified his original statement: —

MY DEAR LAVERY, —

I supposed you were empowered to make me an Honorary Member and then on consenting to your request I became one. Now I hear that Whistler disqualifies Shannon because he belongs to the R.A. . . . I do not wish to be subject to a censorship, and as the same objection applies to me as to

Shannon, I suppose I would be in that case. . . . I prefer to retract my consent if your proposal was not official . . . and that I am in the condition of having given my assent to being proposed and possibly rejected as an R.A. . . . That is what I object to and do not understand. So I prefer to withdraw my consent and remain independent of the International Society, although I have no animosity whatever to it or to its President.

I shall be glad to see you here to-morrow, whether there is anything more to be said about this or not.

Yours sincerely,
JOHN S. SARGENT

He had not forgotten that Whistler's description of him was that of an "acrobat in paint."

When I first went to Paris, in 1881, Sargent was a pupil of Carolus-Duran and divided the honors of the American and French students with Bastien-Lepage, each favoring his own countrymen. The last time I saw him was a couple of weeks before he died, when he was very friendly. When he settled in London he would occasionally come to dinner if Rodin or some such personality was with us, but more often he would refuse. I told him I was painting a crucifix for the lepers at Pretoria, which interested him very much. He had found a wonderful inscription in a church in Italy that he thought might be of use to me. He had used it for his Boston frescoes: —

> Having been made man, I, the Maker of Man,
> And the Redeemer of what I have made;

Having taken on Flesh redeem both flesh
And spirit. For I am God.

He said that he had used the word *redeem* instead of the original *judge*, the Latin being: —

Factus Homo, Factus Hominis,
Factique Redemptor, Judico.

To revert to the International. To attract the public we tried musical afternoons with teas, but Whistler would have none of it and I received a scathing letter about brass bands and buttery teas, negativing our proposal.

Even when the cold forced him south he still kept in touch with the Society by telegram and letter, expecting an instant reply and ignoring possible postal delays. The Mediterranean coast was not hot enough for him, and he wrote to me from Ajaccio, where he had been advised to go for the winter, complaining that I had not written to him and that the climate was not at all satisfactory. But Whistler's real home was 110 Rue du Bac in Paris, once he had left London or, as he put it, "wiped the dust of London off his shoes." He held his court there, and when urgent business about the International had to be considered I would be sent for to consult with him along with Pennell and Sauter.

I remember proposing William Stott, of Oldham, for membership of the International. Whistler did not like him, they came to grips over a model, and when Stott, not wishing to fight, rushed off to Switzerland, Whistler remarked, "Well, he knew he was safe in the land of William Tell and the clock of the sudden cuckoo." Not many months afterwards, going down to Cheyne Walk, where Whistler had returned, I noticed on a poster – "Death of William Stott of Oldham on board ship." I gave the paper to Whistler. "Umph, so he died at sea where he always was." I made some sympathetic remark, to which he replied, "I forgive when I forget."

He had never forgiven Burne-Jones for his evidence on behalf of Ruskin in the famous lawsuit when Whistler claimed £1000 damages and got one farthing from Ruskin for the statement in *Fors Clavigera* – "I have seen and heard much of cockney impudence before now; but never expected to hear a cockscomb ask two hundred guineas for flinging a pot of paint in the public's face." Whistler certainly made a serious error in tactics in this affair. He appealed for damages to his "artistic conscience." That curious man of the world, Bernard Shaw, said to me regarding this, "Whistler shouldn't have wasted his time on his Artistic Conscience. He should have claimed damages on behalf of his commercial reputation and urged an enormous loss of income sustained by Ruskin's attack. That sort of thing can be understood by lawyers, and he would have been awarded £1000. But in talking about his Artistic Conscience he could only raise a farthing – that being all conscience is worth in the eyes of the Law."

On one Varnishing Day at the Salon Burne-Jones had sent his picture "The Depths of the Sea." The critics were enthusiastic, the *Figaro Salon* in large block letters on the front page called him the "Great English Master." On my way to the Rue du Bac I could not help wondering what I should say to the other master. He did not give me a chance; he opened the door with, "Hello, Lavery, what's all this about Mr. Jones?" "Oh," I said, "he has that tall narrow picture of a sailor being pulled down by a mermaid." Whistler still pretended not to know, and I reminded him that it had been in the Academy the previous year. "Dear me, yes, I remember — the unfortunate people in the tank."

A favorite trick of the Master was one that he must have acquired when studying tactics at West Point — the surprise attack. When least expected he would pounce in and upset everything, enjoying the discomfiture produced. A certain artist had been told that Whistler was in Venice with Madame, and he had been introduced to her. Afterwards he was indignant to learn that Madame was a model and swore that he would not speak to Whistler again (all of which was repeated to Whistler). But he must have changed his mind, and one morning, seeing the Master in the Riva degli Schiavoni engaged on one of his etchings, he hailed him with, "Good morning, Mr. Whistler." Without answering Whistler called up to the window, "Maud, Maud, little Robins isn't going to cut us!"

Boldini's portrait, a speaking likeness, did not quite please him. My experience has been that the more truthful the portrait the less is thought of it by the sitter, and

Whistler was no exception to the rule. When I asked him to sit he said, "Oh no, my dear Lavery, I have had enough of that." "Don't you care for the Boldini portrait?" "Well, they tell me it is very like me, but, thank God, I am not like it."

When he got in front of the glass to brush his hair he behaved exactly like a woman settling her permanent wave, placing individual locks, moistened to keep their form, in their allotted places so that they did not interfere with the gray wisp of which he was so proud that stood out of the damp shiny curls on his forehead. His eyebrows were thick and black, his eyes sharp as needles, while a sensitive nose and mouth with prominent chin made up his features. He had beautiful hands, though somewhat clawlike, especially when he would clutch one by the arm to drive home a point. A low, turn-down collar with a narrow black-ribbon bow adorned his wrinkled neck, and his general appearance was that of a small alert ringmaster, whip in hand. I can never remember seeing him, even in the country, in anything other than what are known as court slippers, causing him to be very careful where he stepped out of doors.

One evening he met me on the doorstep as I was going out to dinner. I asked him to come with me, saying that my host would be pleased to see him as he also was a collector of Chinese porcelain. We got to the house; the door of copper, studded with large iron bolts, and the side windows of leaded bottle glass upset him. "Where are you taking me?" Then, putting up his eyeglass and looking me straight in the face, he said, "Here we see the disastrous effect of art on the middle classes." It did not make him better pleased to find that some of the finest pieces in the collection had once been his own property.

He came in one morning to ask me to go to Dieppe with him to see the work of an American woman, – I have forgotten her name, – a pupil of his in his Paris *atelier*, telling me how perfect she was in understanding, and that she would carry on the torch "which I shall hand over when the time comes." I expressed the opinion that no woman was worthy of such an inheritance; why not James Guthrie or Crawhall? "No, they are good in their way, but limited. My dear Lavery, have you never heard of Sappho, or do you know the work of my wife?"

In the National Gallery, where Hogarth was the only English painter to find favor in his eyes, I asked him if there was any one picture that appealed to him especially. He replied at once and without hesitation, "Yes, and here it is." We were already standing in front of the "Milky Way," by Tintoretto. I was interested when I found out afterwards that it was the choice of his late wife.

He was never really the same man after her death. When he stayed with me for a few days at Cromwell Place, I saw a different Whistler from the captious man I had known. No one could have been more considerate or sympathetic. My daughter, aged seven, was home from the Sacred Heart Convent, Roehampton; he called her the "Little Lady of the Holy Heart," and spent hours playing with her doll's house and teaching her amusing rhymes about "a tooter who tooted the flute" and so forth. She adored him, as did my housekeeper, who, he said, ought to be fittingly attired in black silk, and he ordered her a dress at once, giving details as to how it was to be made.

Ten years before, he had saved Eileen's portrait from destruction. It was in "Père et Fille," afterwards purchased for the Luxembourg. I had put it aside for repainting, but catching sight of it in a dark corner of the studio he exclaimed, "What's this? Why, you have at last painted a picture." I wheeled it out into the light and Whistler went over it carefully, examining every inch – it was 7′ x 4′. Then he said, "At last, my dear Lavery, you have done it. It is beautiful. It is complete." I was astonished; it was the first time he had shown any interest in my work.

Very few realize what the placing of a picture in an exhibition means to its author. Years after, in the British-American section of the Luxembourg, I saw this picture in a centre opposite one by Watts. I had never cared much for his painting, but I had to admit he took the shine out of mine. I went back a year afterwards. The pictures had been transposed. I could hardly believe my eyes. The position was reversed. I was in the limelight and he was dull and uninteresting.

The Royal Scottish Academy invited Whistler to

send his portrait of Carlyle to Edinburgh, which he did, pricing it at five hundred guineas. He received a letter asking him if he would be inclined to accept a lower price, stating that as a work of art they were not in favor of its purchase, but as the portrait of a great Scot that would be overlooked. He wired in reply, "The price of the Carlyle is one thousand guineas, dinna ye hear the bagpipes." The following year the picture was exhibited at Glasgow. E. A. Walton got up a petition for its purchase, signed by the Glasgow painters. Sir Frederick Leighton was asked for his name, which he willingly gave, and Whistler's price of a thousand guineas was paid. There was much outcry at the waste of the city's funds, which was quelled by an offer of £10,000 from America. To-day, I believe, £50,000 would not purchase it, unless, perhaps, the civic funds were very low.

He was given an honorary degree by the University; that and the Carlyle recalled to him that the blood of the McNeills of Barra ran in his veins.

Cunninghame Graham wanted to meet him, and I felt very proud of bringing them together. I gave a dinner in a private room at the Metropole Hotel, coming up to London especially for the purpose and inviting everyone I could get hold of, to the number of twenty. Naturally I expected a brilliant evening. But it was a dismal failure. The lambs sat round in open-mouthed silence, ready to drink in the words of wisdom and flow of soul that would come from the lions. But there was no flow –

each wanted his own audience. I could not help remembering the first time that Whistler had dined with me. We were alone. He came at 8 P.M., and I walked halfway home with him at 3 A.M., he talking all the time. I had never heard such talk before, and I doubt if he ever had such an unsophisticated listener. Fresh from Glasgow, which is "no mean city" and where the standard of education is said to be far higher than that of London, I yet had to admit we had no Whistlers. So I had looked forward to the meeting of the two best conversationalists that I knew, only to find that gamecocks are better apart.

Nevertheless, Graham must have been sufficiently interested in Whistler to wish to further his acquaintance, and soon after I arrived in Rome I received a letter from him: –

I hope you are settled in Rome and have seen the Pope, read Zola's *Rome*, and are commencing not to work.

Whistler was immense, I went to his studio and he and I have become great friends.

Crawhall is still wrapped in a mighty and satisfying silence. Who wrote this?

And they heaved a mighty sigh, every soul aboard but me,
As they saw her nose again pointing handsome out to sea,
But all that I could think of in the darkness and the cold,
Was just that I was leaving home and my folks were growing old.

It is from Stevenson's "Christmas at Sea," the best short story in the English language.

When he learned of Whistler's death Graham wrote: –

It was only coming out of Stirling last night that I heard of Whistler's death. Had I known of it in the morning I should have delayed my journey to attend the funeral.

From what you told me I thought the end was near. Well, he was a great man and a great painter, and lived his life and did something. I am always glad to think that from the time of the Old Grosvenor Gallery I had always admired him.

Already the miserable press has begun to damn with faint praise. Let them damn – their rubbish will last to the next edition, but Whistler will remain and his Mother at the Luxembourg be admired when the very names of the hounds who bark are forgotten.

After Whistler's death we held a Memorial Banquet, and I looked to Mr. Choate, the American Ambassador and famed after-dinner speaker, to do justice to the occasion. He flatly refused to speak, saying that he was not going to address experts on a subject of which he was ignorant. In fact, before he would consent to be present, I had to promise that he would not be called upon to speak.

At the dinner, when it was realized that the American Ambassador was going to remain silent, such a noise was made that he had to rise, and, having risen, thrilled everybody by his wonderful oratory. Although the matter was not entirely relevant, the delivery compensated for it.

Next morning Miss Choate was sitting for her portrait at an early hour and I congratulated her on the perfect address by her father the night before. "Yes," she said, "it was pretty good." "What, have you already read it in the papers?" "Why, no, I read it three days ago. You see, my father has such a reputation as an after-dinner speaker that he never goes out unprepared, knowing that he is sure to be called upon to say something. What is really extraordinary is that he never reads what he writes, but visualizes the written word and can give it almost verbatim afterwards. I was interested to know what he had to say about art and so took the manuscript out of the wastepaper basket."

As Mr. Choate refused to preside, we asked Sir Walter Raleigh to do so. He replied: —

I shall be very happy, as I told you to-day by wire, to do what the Society wishes in the matter of toasts. I met Mr. Whistler only twice, I think, and have no personal memories. My interest in painting is that of an amateur, or rather, that of one who is delighted in finding analogies between the arts. But if this is understood, I have a sincere admiration for Mr. Whistler's work and should like to express it. What I can't help feeling is that he must mean more for many of the company than ever he would mean to me. You can't understand an art you don't practise — never.

Whistler gone, we invited Rodin to be President of the International Society. He wrote to accept, saying: —

Mr. Vice President, —

I am very grateful for the honor you have paid me in

offering me the Presidency of the International Society of Sculptors, Painters, and Gravers of London, and I beg you to receive my acceptance.

In expressing to you the interest with which I will follow the movements of the Society, I beg you, Mr. Vice President, to receive the assurance of my feelings of highest consideration.

AUGUSTE RODIN

I think he only came to London on three occasions during his Presidency, and then he spent all his time in the British Museum. Every fragment of Greek sculpture appealed to him, he thought no other museum had such a collection. I mentioned the "Victory of Samothrace" at the Louvre as being the most wonderful example of any art in existence, but he said he preferred the British Museum group of two women from the Parthenon.

He was a little, strongly built man of about five foot six, with broad shoulders. My portrait of him in the Tate Gallery gives an impression of a taller man, because of his being placed too high on the canvas.

Each year, not wishing to be entirely outdone by the Academy, we gave a banquet, entertaining as our guest of honor a foreign ambassador. Whistler was not enthusiastic about the idea, and I cannot remember his ever presiding at one; but by the time of his death the function had become something of an institution. It was a little embarrassing for Rodin to have to entertain the German Ambassador at that time. But he sent a letter for me to read in his absence: —

We have received great encouragement, and if warm approbations accompany us still more to-day, it is to our artists that the merit is due . . . they are worthy to be supported by their efforts. . . . The artist, like the poet, more intensely alive to all things about him, begins like him to discover the entire world of beauty. Observation, the essential and primordial science, reveals all Nature to him . . . and sincere knowledge is already identical with the most profound admiration. . . . To discover all things in beauty intact is to recover the thousands of blessings that have from the beginning been prepared for us.

The artist recovers from bare Nature all the elements of eternal Art. With him artistic thought quits the palace of the ideal, feeling himself there too sumptuously confined, in order to return to the earliest text of God. It is, perhaps, that effort which has procured numerous sympathies for our Society, for at bottom everyone is waiting for those simple and human artists who will demonstrate clearly and forcibly that beauty is not the exception, that she is everywhere around us and each one of us may share in her without leaving the place of his humble task.

We open our doors always to true artists of all countries, and willingly accept as proof that our efforts are understood abroad, the inestimable presence of His Excellency, the Ambassador of Germany, whose acceptance of our invitation to this banquet has added another title of honor to our Society to those previously conferred by Ambassadors of other nations.

Poor Rodin had not much luck with his own people. His secretary, Mademoiselle Judith Cladel, in her biography of the Master, tells many tales of his vicissitudes. One stays in my mind. When his "Age of Bronze" came before the Salon jury it was rejected on the ground that it was cast from life. The work was so perfect as to deceive experts. In fact, his life was a record of ignorant misunderstanding. He loved London and gave some fifty of his most important works in bronze to the Victoria and Albert Museum, where they were specially placed.

From the first day I entered the cast room of the Glasgow School of Art I have been in love with sculpture, so much so that it never occurred to me that I could become a sculptor – my few attempts satisfied me on that point. My joy can be imagined when one day in Rodin's studio he offered me the choice of any of his bronzes in exchange for a painting. I have often been offered exchange of work by brother painters and as often have got out of it on some excuse or other. Not because I did not appreciate the offer, but from a feeling that I had as many pictures of my own filling up my studio as I wanted. The passion of possession, even of masterpieces, has never been one of my weaknesses.

I am told I only see sculpture as a painter. Be that as it may, I prefer Epstein's "Rima" in the Park to the Albert Memorial! Once at a dinner party when London sculpture was being discussed, – I think it was *chez* Lady Colefax, – Edwin Lutyens leant across the table and in his playful manner said, "John, I hear you are defending

'Rima.' " "My dear Edwin, I have done worse than that. I have been defending the Cenotaph." He did not let me go free, but I remember the incident because he is difficult to score off.

XI

HAZEL AND ALICE

IN 1904 I had such a success with "Spring" that I decided to paint the seasons. I was looking for a spot to paint "Summer" when I had a letter from J. Milner Kite, an Anglo-French-American painter, inviting me to go to Brittany. So, thinking it might solve the problem of the picture, I went to Beg-mai, taking with me "Spring," the little German girl, and Shiel, an Irishman with nothing to do. After working all day from a model in the country it has always been a relief to me to have a third person, male or female, to take the sitter off my hands, so to speak, and reduce the strain for both model and painter. Shiel served my purpose in that he shared the scandal, if there should be one, of my taking a beautiful girl to the country for months at a time.

Staying in the same hotel were two girls whom I used to see on their veranda at morning coffee, as I passed on my way to work with my six-foot canvas strapped to my shoulders. Kite informed me that they were Americans with their mother, and that he was trying to paint the elder one, who, I could see, was very beautiful; and he added that he would be forever indebted to me if I could give him a hand. I was only too glad to show off, especially before such loveliness, and as it is invariably much easier to work on another man's canvas when he has got into difficulties than it is on one's own under similar circumstances, in a very short time I was looked upon by the sitter as a master and treated with great respect, not to say admiration. I cannot say that I was appreciated by the mother, whom Kite called "the old Chicago dame" – which I thought disrespectful, since she had commissioned him to paint her daughter.

Mrs. Edward Jenner Martyn was not in sympathy with Bohemians, but she had come to an artists' colony in France at the request of her eldest daughter, Hazel, who had a talent for drawing that was quite masterly. She was about seventeen and possessed the largest and most heavenly eyes I had ever seen. She came from Chicago, with the reputation of being the most brilliant and beautiful girl in the Middle West. She had just had a *succès fou* with an exhibition of drawings and etchings. She herself was extremely modest about her work, and even apologetic.

In the evenings, after the dinner things had been cleared, Mrs. Martyn, Hazel, and her sister Dorothy, with Kite, Shiel, Mary, and myself, plus another young man called Pompey Howard, who was not an artist but had followed the Martyn family from Paris in order to advance his unsuccessful attentions on Hazel, would gather round the table. Mrs. Martyn had her knitting and her sharp American eye on the company. The exquisite little Dorothy, whose destiny it was to be outshone by the still greater lights of her sister, dived deep down into a book, pretending to have not the slightest interest in the art talk which the rest of us endlessly carried on.

I cannot understand to this day what Hazel saw in me – she said I reminded her of Harry Lauder. I was more than twice her age; I was traveling with a model (it is true that Kite and Shiel were with us). I was a widower with a daughter almost as old as herself. I was Irish, to her a nationality associated with Tammany Hall, and she was already engaged to a young surgeon, son of the famous Dr. Trudeau at whose sanatorium Robert Louis Stevenson was an impatient inmate, breaking up his furniture to make a fire in the intense cold which eventually drove him to Honolulu. Mrs. Martyn, observing the interest her daughter was showing in me, sent Trudeau a message to come at once or he would lose Hazel. He came, he observed, and he married her.

I then realized that painting pictures was not everything.

Three or four months afterwards Trudeau died suddenly. In the course of time Alice was born and Hazel returned to Paris with her child, who, at the age of five, acted as bridesmaid with Dorothy when, with Cunninghame Graham as my best man, I married her mother at Brompton Oratory.

Just about the time when Hazel and Alice came into my life I bought a little property on the hill outside

Tangier, known to Moors as Dar-el-Midfah because of a derelict cannon half buried in the front garden. I made it my winter quarters for the next fifteen or more years, Hazel at the start being twenty-three and Alice five. I remember the latter's age well. I was painting a portrait of Kenneth Clark, – the present Director of the National Gallery, – who was then aged six or seven, and Alice came up to the studio to entertain the sitter. The dialogue was pretty good.

HE. Hello, who are you?

SHE. I am Alice.

HE. How old are you?

SHE. I've just struck five.

HE. Did you ting or did you cuckoo?

When she went to school she was asked by her companions why her name was Trudeau and her mother's Lavery. She was much embarrassed, and swallowing hard said, "Well, you see, my mother married a friend of mine, and that's how it came about." This was literally true, because I had promised to marry her when she grew up. When I married her mother she said resignedly, "Well, we'll just have to be friends."

On our last day at Wengern I had to finish my "Japanese Switzerland" – Hazel and Alice in the snow – and they were very patient; but as time went on and Alice saw how little of it would be left for a run on her luge, I overheard her say to her mother, "Isn't it a pity, Muffie, that we married an artist?"

Although I spent some winters in Morocco, she

picked up the language much quicker than I did. What is more, living in the stables in Tangier she acquired stable Arabic with equal facility. One day riding Moses, her donkey, she was heard addressing him in Arabic with, "Go on, thou son of an adulteress," and similar epithets.

The domestic question in Morocco was a difficult one, since a Moor lost caste if he or she served a Christian; but I had the luck to get two remarkable characters, one Aïsha, a girl of about sixteen, and the other Ben Ali Rabbati, a cook and also an artist in water colors. When Aïsha came she could only speak Spanish and Arabic; within a month her English was wonderful. She preferred to call herself Aïda because it sounded Spanish. I painted a picture of her which I sent to the Venice Triennale Esposizione di Belle Arti. The King of Italy paid a visit, and among other pictures purchased that of Aida. It was reproduced as a frontispiece in *Illustrazione Italiana*. Aïda was very proud of it and made good use of it in London.

She used to take Alice out in the Park, where a young German poet became interested in her. We later found out that he was mad, but she had already told him that she was related to the Italian Royal House, in proof of which she showed her portrait in the Italian journal under which was printed: "Aïda, from the collection of His Majesty the King." She explained to the poet that she was a Moorish princess and that I had smuggled her out of Morocco and was treating her like a slave. He was much impressed, and when he had got all her facts he wrote to *Truth* to expose what he called "Brown Slave Traffic in Our Midst."

I had had difficulty in getting her out of Morocco, it being against the law for a Moorish woman to leave the country, but Sir Reginald Lister, the last British Minister, came to my aid by assuring the Basha she would be brought back safely. She was dressed up in my daughter's European clothes, heavily veiled, and the high-heeled shoes made her walk strangely. She was very sick in the small boat going out to the steamer, and her not daring to remove the tightly tied veil made it even more embarrassing. The boatman had suspicions which a few dollars allayed, and we got safely on board the P. & O. liner. When the time came to go back, however, she refused, saying, "Me free under British flag." I was told at the Foreign Office that I could not force her to return unless she became an undesirable alien, so we had to go back without her, in great fear of the trouble her family would make. When we told them they merely said, "Poison awaits her, which, Allah be praised, will be sure."

Soon after our return the War broke out, and Aïda disappeared, to be found in a munition factory. In a few months she had charge of a number of workers, and at the end of the War she married the manager of her department.

Ben Ali is a messenger in the Tangier branch of the Bank of Spain, and for some years at Christmas he sent me a water color of much merit depicting a Moorish scene. He is the only Moorish artist I know of whose work is not entirely geometrical and yet is purely Moorish. He was an excellent cook and, unlike the Christianized Moor, strictly honest. His best work was signed, "Done by Allah through his servant, Ben Ali."

The winter of 1920 was our last in Morocco. Hazel expressed a desire to see the interior, so we got a couple of "tin Lizzies," a Spanish and an Arab chauffeur who could cook, and set off – Hazel, Alice, Mary Black Hawkins, Nora Kerr-Clark, the sister of the British Consul, and myself! The evening before starting we dined with Sir Menebi. When we told him we were off the next day for Marrakesh and Fez he said, "My palaces in both cities are yours and will be ready for you when you arrive." Since the French occupation, or what was called the *entente cordiale*, Menebi refused to be in residence in either city. We were met in Marrakesh by an army of slaves who shouldered our luggage, the streets being too narrow to admit passage in a car without blocking everything else. We were received with great ceremony in a marble courtyard with an immense fountain throwing up tons of water, surrounded by orange trees in bloom and laden with fruit, and then ushered into a palatial room with divans and an immense bed. It was taken for granted that the four ladies were my wives. Alice, being the youngest, was treated with especial respect.

We sat down to an endless meal, rose water being

handed round to dip the fingers in after each course; then coffee and a variety of sweetmeats were served, while two dancing girls appeared and the strange, monotonous Oriental music that had accompanied the feast grew strident. We were all getting cramped and tired when Hazel, not wishing Alice to see the contortions of the dancers, said, "For heaven's sake, John, ask where our bedrooms are." I knew just enough Arabic to make this known to the Halifa. His answer was, "This is your bedroom, my lord!" I was in the harem.

Later, El Glowi, who was really more powerful than the Sultan, sent a messenger and his chief eunuch to invite the ladies of my harem to visit his.

I have asked Alice to write her experiences, and this is what she wrote: –

After the most sumptuous repast El Glowi asked if the ladies would like to visit his "household" that afternoon. It was apparently indelicate to allude to his wives or family as anything but his "household."

And a household it proved to be – between 200 and 300 women, and goodness knows how many children and slaves. They had a palace to themselves in a different part of the city to that of their Lord and Master. El Glowi's superabundance of wives was due to the fact that he had recently inherited his brother-in-law's harem. I have never seen anything like the color and beauty of that crowd of shy yet curious women who came across the sunlit courtyard to meet us, nervous and excited as no modern schoolchildren would be. Arrayed in their best like a flock of birds of Paradise, they whispered and giggled.

Only three of the women stood out as possessing separate personalities – El Glowi's principal wife, Lala Rahman, his brother-in-law's chief wife, and a little Circassian girl, so lovely that even surrounded by beauty she could not pass unnoticed. Milk-white skin, jet-black hair, and long black lashes over eyes of a real, deep periwinkle blue, cheeks and lips as bright as, and fresher than, any cosmetics could make them. We asked her age through the interpreters and were staggered by the reply, "Just thirteen!"

In all the gay crowd Lala Rahman alone wore black, with the usual white muslin overgarment, broad black and silver belt, and no jewels. We asked was she in mourning? She was, not for anyone deceased, but for her own tragic life. She was barren and had failed to please her Lord and Master, and was being returned to the house of her father, Sir Menebi. Her beauty was pale and patient like that of the cloistered nun and there was no reproach in her gentle brown eyes: sorrow had wrapped her in its shroud and raised her beyond the mundane gayety of her companions. How strange it seems that in this age a girl still lives who broke her heart before she was twenty because she could not bear a child.

Her successor was of a very different cast. Yellow-skinned, smooth with a bloom like a nectarine; long, upward-slanting eyes, heavy-lidded; a small proud head – how the film producers would have gobbled her up – the super vamp! She had dress sense too, purple and gold, and a high pearl choker on her slender neck, immense single-stone rings on her long henna-stained fingers.

We had the usual sweet mint tea and sickly biscuits, and all the time we were plied with eager questions. I remember what amazed them most was the fact I was Mother's child. How could that be? Again and again they pointed naïvely at Mother's stomach and then at me: was it really true I came out of her? By twenty-five they would be old women: like flowers of a day they bloom and fade and have no lasting. We asked them if they ever went out. Yes, once a year, to the cemetery, they said; but as they belonged to such a powerful rich man they went completely veiled without even one eye uncovered, led on mules by slaves. Asked about their lord they said quite simply that he came to them in the evenings, that he was most amused by his black concubines whom he kept until they were quite old because they made him laugh, whereas once a beautiful woman got old she simply bored him and he either sold her or gave her away. They said they had communal wardrobes and jewel chests, and spent their time cooking, dressing up, and playing with and minding their children. They seemed happy and uncomplicated in their outlook. They were beaten when they quarreled with each other, they lived for each day as it came, looking for and wanting nothing more than they had because they had never known any other kind of life, and they were content, much more content than many others who have the whole world to wander over in search of peace and happiness.

The children were running around all this time paying very little attention to us, intent on their games of "tig" and "hide-and-seek," and the fat black concubines were shaking with mirth and the exertion of chasing them.

Then we rose to go after much bowing and thanking and exchange of politenesses. Imagine our surprise, which later turned to alarm, when a huge black eunuch barred our way saying that he had orders from his Master not to let us out until he came. The Scottish interpretress got very anxious and said such a thing had never happened before. It was unheard of that El Glowi or any other Moor should be seen with his household in the presence of visitors, especially Christians. Miss Kerr-Clark nearly had hysterics, the place became as noisy as a rookery, and it was my mother who got us out after an hour of arguing. She tried everything unsuccessfully and then struck on the idea of appealing to them on their own ground. "I have a Lord and Master too, and if I am kept here he will be furious and punish me. Now, if you let us out at once we promise you to see your Lord and explain the matter to him and see that you do not get beaten." They understood and trustingly let us go.

As we passed along the narrow dark passage out into the street I heard a cry and looked into a dimly lit room. I saw a young girl, huddled in a corner, with upraised arms; a eunuch, like a bronze statue, stripped to the waist, was standing over her, whip in hand, ready to punish with the unemotional deliberation of his kind. I had a curious feeling of indifference about the matter, as if my slight acquaintance with the Oriental wife had made me realize that such things must be borne like children and pain and death.

We passed El Glowi's entourage in the narrow street. Mother said, "What a blessing we got out in time. I know John would have refused to pay the ransom!"

XII

THE WAR YEARS

ARRIVING in Dublin in the early morning of August 4, 1914, on a jaunting car, I found the newspaper boys running through the streets shouting. I asked the driver to stop for a paper. "Sure, it's the races they're after calling." We got a paper and he was right. Later in the day we knew that catastrophe had arrived. We went back by the night boat to find London in an uproar. St. James's Park was already an armed camp, of which I made my first war picture. Then in a very short space of time "The First Wounded in London Hospital, August 1914," now in the Municipal Gallery, Dundee. The outcry against Germany was indescribable. I found myself in a very awkward corner: an Irishman – it is true I was from Belfast – making his way in the London he loved in spite of its assurance and superiority complex, that are sometimes trying, and where he was honored by Englishmen; a pacifist without the moral courage of a Bernard Shaw or a Ramsay MacDonald, and one, besides, having German sympathies, since there I had been looked on as one of the greatest painters and overwhelmed with commissions.

Now was the time to run with the hare and hunt

with the hounds. I did it by joining the Artists' Rifles and drilling in the quadrangle of Burlington House and at Earl's Court, where a corner was given us. One afternoon I was late for drill and joined the people looking on at the corps in grubby white jerseys by way of uniform. Rather a scrubby lot of painters, sculptors, actors, musicians, hairdressers, scene shifters, and so on, of all ages. Listening to the comments of the crowd, I heard the following: "What are they?" "Don't you know? Why, they're German prisoners. Aren't they awful?" The second or third route march did for me. I had to call in the doctor, whose verdict was, "My dear sir, go back to your paintpots, you will do more for your country with your brush than with your rifle." I knew he was right. I got a great deal of interest out of it all. I could see why men in the real army were so keen – or appeared so to me – to face death. It was a fine sensation to feel that all responsibility of living had been taken from you, that all the worries of house and home had ceased to exist. You were walking on air to the tune of "It's a long way to Tipperary," and nothing mattered. The intoxication was complete for the time being.

Our first march to the country was on a lovely Sunday morning, all singing at the top of our voices, women waving from their windows and wishing us Godspeed. Crowds of children followed us in the streets, not much impressed by the baldheaded men and anaemic youths that formed our corps. When the obviously old were passing they would call out, "Now, young 'un, step up," or, "When are they going to burn ye?" – the latter borrowed from propaganda. I soon began to see that years do tell; up till that time I had believed myself equal to, if not more fit than, some of the youths I formed fours with. In the end they went to the trenches and I went to bed. It was surprising to see how quickly they responded to discipline and turned from B3 class recruits into A1 soldiers.

What I really wanted to do was to go to the Front to paint, so I saw Mr. Masterman, who was in charge of propaganda and at once offered me a commission. I set about getting my painting outfit, of which I was very proud, and a motor van to live in, all the time feeling that Hazel's objections would be very hard to overcome when she knew my intentions. As it was, I could never be out of her sight a minute, so I decided that when everything was ready I would say nothing and wire when I was safely on board the transport. But it was not to be. At the last minute, one night in the darkness, we had a disastrous accident in Park Lane. We were carried into St. George's Hospital, where it was found that Hazel had severe concussion and I a milder form. When our wounds were dressed we were taken home in an ambulance, where she lay in bed for a year. I was able to move about the house only by leaving the room when she slept, her obsession that I would be run over being so strong. Finally the doctor insisted that I should get out of doors, if only for an hour. A curious thing happened. I had been out for half an hour or so when gradually my mind became blank and I did not know where I was. I had a vague notion that I was walking in a street in Rome, and at the same time I wanted to get back to Hazel. I tried to speak to people, but they did not seem to understand and passed on. I knew that there was something wrong, and I had an indescribable fear. If only I could get a cup of tea, I thought, it would be all right. I went up one street and down another, all strange; then, terribly exhausted, I found myself sitting alone at a marble-topped table in the refreshment room at Gloucester Road Station, ten minutes' walk from home.

Fortunately the doctor had stayed with Hazel, explaining to her that I was asleep in the next room. When I returned, some three hours later, he told me he had had to give her an injection as she had become so hysterical. For some days he was a bit anxious about me. I had acute insomnia, which he thought to help by hypnotism. I still hoped that with his help I could get to the Front, but it was useless. He said, "If you want to hasten your wife's death, go."

Now opportunely came an invitation from the Duke of Westminster inviting us to his shooting lodge in the Landes. As usual Hazel would not move without the "whole dam' family." She had strange courage – if either Alice or I crossed the threshold she was in agony until the wanderer got back, yet if the *three* of us had been invited to the Western Front she would have accepted the invitation.

We got to Paris in safety – and what a Paris! Dirty streets, shutters up, miserable people, mostly old men and women, obvious foreigners at the cafés on the *grands boulevards*. Everyone looked sad. How different from London, where a grim, don't-care look prevailed with "Business As Usual" staring you in the face everywhere. I thought that at any rate there was the Latin Quarter, and my old haunts where I might come across a friendly face, but it was as if a deadly plague had swept the place – scarcely a living thing was to be seen. I hurried away and sought my old friend Jacques Émile Blanche, at no time a very gay dog but the most cultivated and the kindliest of men. I could think of no one else that Hazel knew. We were ushered into the studio – it also had a standstill look and a feeling of desolation.

A door opened. There stood Blanche, and in a voice a little above a whisper he said, "Ah, my dear Lavery, and Madame, how kind of you!" Then, seeing that Hazel and Alice were in summer dresses, he said in a severely disapproving voice, "French ladies dress in black at this time." I tried to change the subject and said cheerfully, "I expect you have sent a great masterpiece to the Salon." Deeply resentful came the reply, "Ah, you English do not know what we French are going through. It is hell. There is no Salon. No one paints."

We hastened away from this dead Paris to Mimisau, a small château in the middle of a lake, where, for a short time, we were able to forget the War, and Hazel recovered her normal health.

On my return to London I received a note from Orpen, who wrote from the Front: –

MY DEAR LAVERY, –

A sudden impulse makes me write to you – I have been thinking (a strange thought) I heard you wanted to come out here to work and that you were coming – but so far as I know you have not done so yet. Having now a vast experience of the Army, my "thinking" brought me to the conclusion that very probably the "Army" had said you could not come out until I returned. I wonder, did they?

Anyhow I would be very glad if you would let me know. There is no reason in the wide world why you should not be here as well – the car I use is not one of their cars, but one I got through the Q.M.G. and brought over myself on the steamer – so I write this letter in case you have "rotten" thoughts about me.

I had a grand time with Maurice Baring – and I think his "In Memoriam" is a masterpiece.

Do come out, Lavery, I think you would like it – but it's so vast and overpowering it is difficult to grasp anything.

Please give my love to Mrs. Lavery and the same to yourself.

I remain,
WILLIAM ORPEN

I wrote to him and explained all the circumstances and received a full-page caricature of himself painting at the Front and a letter in reply: –

My dear Lavery, –

Many thanks for your letter. I was afraid some of these blighters might have been making out to you that I was preventing your coming out – but now I know that all is well – I'll try to take care of myself all right – of all the blinking funks that ever lived I'm the worst – my stomjack just gets tied up in knots – and I get a great longing to dig myself in at once.

My love to Mrs. Lavery and yourself.

Yours,
Orpen

I had always admired Orpen from the first day I saw a picture of his in the New Gallery – a bedroom with a chaise longue on which an elegant lady reclined. It was a portrait of Rosie Boote, afterwards Lady Headfort, and I wrote congratulating him, saying that there was only one flaw – that the signature was "Orpen" and not "Lavery." In 1918 Hazel and I went to Agnew's to see his war pictures in oil and water color, all in white frames, giving the impression of brightness even to some of the grim war scenes that were interspersed with a series of brilliant portraits of generals, a German prisoner or two mingling with the Tommies, and all touched with his inimitable brush. There was one pathetic picture of a beautiful girl looking unutterably sad, a tear glistening in her eye. He told us he had been given permission to paint her in prison the day before she faced the firing squad as a German spy. He asked us not to mention this to anyone, as if it got out he might get into trouble. It did get out, and he did get into trouble with the French authorities. A couple of months afterwards, in Paris, we went to *déjeuner* at Henry's. There at a table we saw Orpen and the "German spy," a very pretty little *midinette*. She was his model and he was the "firing squad."

No British painter since Hogarth has ridiculed people in power so effectively as Orpen has done. Witness his two masterpieces of the "Versailles Treaty," the most powerful historical documents of the age and at the same time great works of art. Having finished with the "war to end war," he finished up with the treaty to prolong it.

The first war picture that really interested me was "The Kensingtons at Levantie," by Eric Kennington, a private in the 13th London Regiment – a mere boy in the trenches, I was told. Shortly afterwards I was having my hair cut. Sitting in the chair next to mine was a sunburnt young man undergoing the same process. In the looking glass I could see he was trying to catch my eye. Finally, having made up his mind, he nodded, saying all in one breath and without waiting for an answer, "Are you Lavery? My name is Kennington. You know my father. I want to get back to the Front to paint, and you can help me." I believe he got his wish. He had one thing in common with Orpen that attracted me – exceptional technical ability.

Later came C. R. W. Nevinson, private, R.A.M.C., with his surprising aeroplanes and perhaps the most terrifying picture of the War, "The Harvest of Battle." Then John Nash, with "Oppy Wood. Evening, 1917." His brother Paul, with the "Marne Road." The works of these three young painters bring home to the spectators as vividly as any pictures I have seen the hideousness and horrors of war. Finishing up with "An Advanced Dressing-Station in France, 1918," by my old friend the late Professor Henry Tonks. It is somewhat invidious to mention names. I do not mean that these are the only painters worthy of consideration, but that they, among others, appeal to me as excellent propaganda for peace.

I realized that for a painter mine was a "cushy" job when I learnt of Philip Connard, whose courage in taking on submarine work and frequently going into action made me feel like those patriots who sit at home dauntlessly courageous in the face of the other fellow's danger.

After my efforts to get to France had failed, an order came from the Admiralty to make records on canvas of the naval bases. My first experience was behind the Forth Bridge, where the Fleet was at anchor. I had a general permit enabling me to pass anywhere, but no sooner had I got to work than I was stopped by the local police and marched off to Headquarters. They thought the permit too good to be true, but they found it all right and I was released. But I had been seen in the hands of the police, and children who had been told to look for spies became troublesome, calling me "the German spy painting oor brig," and throwing stones. Petty officers and sailors were always wanting to see my permit, and finally I said to one jaunty young man, "Can you tell me how many of you people have the right to interfere with me?" He smiled and said, "Well, I think we must be about fifty thousand."

The next time I visited the Forth was to paint Admiral Beatty dictating terms to Admiral Meurer in the *Queen Elizabeth*. I had received orders to be on board by a certain date, and I spent the night with Admiral Jellicoe on shore. The morning was cold and foggy, making it difficult to reach the flagship. The German delegates were due to arrive at 11 A.M., but owing to the fog, mutiny, and coal shortage, the surrendered Fleet did not reach anchorage until 4 P.M. Meanwhile I had been preparing two studies: first, the arrival on the quarter-deck. The fog and darkness blotted out the detail, making it comparatively easy to get a quick impression. The second was more complicated — a close-up of the scene in the fore-cabin. As I was in mufti a uniform had to be found for me. The Commodore dressed me up in a post captain's discarded uniform that happened to fit. My painting things were hidden behind flowers on a side table, where I was unobserved by the delegates.

I got a fairly good impression of the arrival on the quarter-deck and rushed down to the fore-cabin after the delegates, but not in time to see their reception by the British Admirals, which did not take long. They were already seated when I took up my position, the door was closed, and the proceedings began. Most people would have been all ears, but I was all eyes and heard very little, except for once or twice when the German Admiral, who spoke perfect English, corrected an interpreter on some idiomatic point. Not to embarrass the delegates, I chose a place behind them where what I was doing could not be seen, even if they should turn round, which the Zeppelin commander occasionally did, being nearest to me. He was a young man of the Prussian type, with closely cropped hair and flat back to his head. He evidently felt his position keenly and was ill at ease. The Admiral, whose profile I could see at times and who did most of the talking, might have been an Englishman; his demeanor was dignified, but one could tell by his voice the strain under which he was laboring. The submarine commander next to him was somewhat aggressive if not defiant when he spoke, which was seldom. The end delegate I could not see.

They had dinner on board, and the meeting was adjourned until the following morning at eleven. I stood at attention and saluted as they filed out, blocking any chance of my canvas being seen. There was still a fairly dense fog the next morning, which was lucky for me as the lighting had changed very little. I did not trouble much about our side, knowing that I could get sittings later on. The adjourned meeting lasted some hours — I did all I could in the time, and the result may be seen in the War Museum. I thought Admiral Beatty somewhat severe on the fallen foe. I was much relieved when he turned to Admiral Tyrwhitt, saying, "I know you have many things to attend to, Admiral, and now that your section is complete [they had been dealing with submarines and mine fields for about three hours] you may go or stay as you please." He rose, saluted, and passed into the outer cabin; I slipped out behind him without saluting, having forgotten that I was in uniform. I had been working at fever heat for eight hours and was dog-tired. When the door closed, Tyrwhitt said with a sigh, "I am damned sorry for those fellows." I have always liked sailors and the sea, the latter from the shore. "Lavery of the Waves," according to Cunninghame Graham, is the English translation of my name; I have not been able to live up to it, except by painting a few sea pieces.

When I saw Orpen's treatment of "Versailles," my "Surrender of the Fleet" appeared to me totally uninspired and dull as dishwater, as did my other war pictures. Instead of the grim harshness and horror of the scenes I had given charming color versions, as if painting a bank holiday on Hampstead Heath. Escorting convoys in the North Sea and painting from "blimps" or numbered N.S.'s, I felt nothing of the stark reality, losing sight of my fellow men being blown to pieces in submarines or slowly choking to death in mud. I saw only new beauties of color and design as seen from above, and the excitement of getting ready to bomb a submarine which as often as not was a whale coming up to blow. This actually happened on one occasion. "All Clear for Action" was given, and I looked over the side;

right beneath, deep down in the sea, I could make out a green object slowly coming to the surface and two white waterspouts appeared. It was a whale blowing.

Early in the same year I started off in midwinter from London in the naval train for the far North, with thoughts of Switzerland and how simple to paint people in snow in sunshine. But when I got into talk with my companions, who were intrigued and wondered what a man in mufti could be doing amongst them, I explained that I was an artist going to Scapa Flow to make pictures. They were astonished, one saying, "My God, fancy going there from choice." They described the crossing through "Hell's Gate" from Thurso for my edification, no doubt exaggerating the number of wrecks and the impossibility of rescue in fogs, rushing currents, and rocks, which made navigation terrifying. The day wore on with an occasional stop to clear the snow off the rails, and as darkness was settling down we ran into a drift and were held up for hours and told there was a train on another line in the same plight from the day before. At long last we got to Thurso, stiff with cold, but happy at the thought of a hotel and a pint of champagne. I never could touch whiskey. We plunged through the snow to the hotel, a temperance one with an icy-cold coffee room, a black smoking fire giving out no heat, and a blue-nosed decrepit waiter shuffling about. "Hell's Gate" would be open at 4 A.M., so a hot-water bottle and bed without undressing were my only choice, with a hot cup of bad coffee. The next thing I remember was being bundled into an open car with my painting outfit and a couple of heavy batteries for the electrified suit which had been taken off a German airman and would enable me to stand the biting winds when I was at work. I thought I knew what cold meant when standing painting in the snow in Switzerland. I didn't.

We were to pick up an officer on the way to the little pier, and in the five minutes we waited the wind was so strong that the car had to be dug out of a snowdrift before we could move. When we got to the pier I knew what was meant by "Hell's Gate." In the darkness and blinding snow I could only make out shadowy figures, muffled up, scrambling backward and forward, clinging to ropes and carrying things. One was bawling orders through a megaphone, and I tried to get at him, holding on to anything I could catch. It was too dangerous. The pier was a sheet of black glittering ice, and the wind swept everything before it. I made up my mind to go back. Hazel had begged me not to undertake such an expedition at my age, telling me that I was a fool. I saw she was right. I tried to get someone in command to order the unloading of my outfit, which was already on board. In the rush and scuffle it was impossible to distinguish one man from another. Seeing the hopelessness of it all, and that there was no retreat, I got on board. At the base of the funnel the ice was melting, showing the brown of the rusty metal. I missed my footing and rolled down the companionway to the deck. Scrambling to a bench under cover, I lay down, prepared for the worst. In what I took to be ten minutes a blinding light was thrown on my face, waking me up. It was the morning sun gleaming through a porthole. I had been asleep for three hours and did not know it! All was quiet except for the gentle rolling of the boat. The storm had passed, leaving a rippling prismatic sea, with the low, snow-covered hills of Scapa sparkling in the sun. I was dazed with delight – it was *Heaven's* Gate. To think that I had feared it, and but for the fact that I could not go back might have been dubbed a weakling. Cowardice and courage are often indistinguishable, and it is a terrible thought that often the coward passes for a brave man and is placed on a pedestal when courage goes unrewarded. Courage, like virtue, must often be its own reward. The beautiful scene did not last, the wind came again, and before night I knew nothing could live out of doors on those bare rocks. My electrified suit was no use without shelter; there was no standing against the wind. I did, however, manage to bring back two or three color sketches that are now in the War Museum.

After four days there was a chance of getting back to the mainland – a batch of naval ratings were going on leave. It was a bright morning and there was great joy when we put off. The merriment was at its height when, halfway over, we were enveloped in a fog so dense that nothing was to be seen, and just as suddenly silence, save for the faint sound of rushing currents and swirling waters, reigned supreme. If we were to be dashed on a rock and drowned in the darkness we should all go together, and, strange to say, the thought was almost consoling. However, before it could be put to the test the fog lifted and the voices rose in redoubled energy — not in prayer, I fear.

From beginning to end, bar a little discomfort at times, I saw or felt nothing of the horrors of war excepting perhaps "The First Wounded in London Hospital, 1914," and listening to their tales whilst I painted it. Later on, when the German prisoners were coming in, I could not help sympathizing with their forlorn look of hopelessness. In some cases, if I had dared, I should have spoken to them or made them some kindly sign that in England we were not all out for their blood; but I let them pass on, chastened by the thought that, perhaps, they were no worse off than British soldiers in Germany — as if that would help matters. What was striking as the War went on was that the bitterest feelings were not expressed by the soldiers in the trenches or by those who came back, but by the civilians in their comfortable homes, especially the useless, miserable ones whose loud-mouthed patriotism proclaimed their desire to fight to the last. There were a few who spoke of fighting our own family, saying that when all was said and done we were Anglo-Saxons; and many, I felt, thought this but were afraid to say it. I remember at a fashionable dinner table "Lord Tommy," as he was known to his friends, asserting that there were people that he disliked more than the Germans, and they were the French. The people I disliked most were the amateur spy-hunters. It may have been that the one or two I happened to know in private life were very objectionable people who would not have been tolerated in peace-time in any society, but who, during the War, managed to squeeze themselves into positions where they often caused much suffering to innocent people and rarely did any good.

Perhaps what struck me as the worst thing during the War were the lists of the missing. Unfortunately, two very dear friends of Hazel's, Lord Basil Blackwood and Lord Alexander Thynne, appeared in these lists. These two inseparables went out together to the Front. In due course they came back, both severely wounded. As they had done their bit, everyone was surprised to hear them express a fear that the War Office would not allow their return to the trenches – not that they had any blood-thirsty desires but simply because of the sheer boredom of inaction at home.

They were both admirers of Hazel and complained bitterly that they could never see her alone. If either called in the afternoon at Cromwell Place he was sure to find the other there. One evening at a dinner they were giving vent to their woes when Mr. Asquith, the Prime Minister, remarked that he found the Diploma Gallery at Burlington House the most perfect place for an assignation.

This gave Alex an idea, which resulted in his making an appointment with Hazel to meet him in the Central

Hall of the South Kensington Museum. She kept him waiting half an hour and rushed up to apologize. He, without speaking, desiring to punish her, turned on his heel and strode off while she, surprised and indignant, ran after him trying to speak. The Museum attendants were looking on, and it flashed through her mind that she might be accused of trying to accost a strange gentleman in a public place. She redoubled her efforts to keep up with him, catching him by the arm, which he pulled away. This was too much – she burst into tears and he into laughter.

Basil and he got their wish and returned to the trenches. They were never more heard of, and Hazel was glad she had forgiven Alex before he left.

XIII

REFLECTIONS ON PORTRAIT PAINTING

ONCE, congratulating Rodin on the extraordinary likeness in bronze he had made of Puvis de Chavannes, Geffroy Dubois, Mercié, Falguière, and a number of others, he replied to me, "You will scarcely believe it, but some of the men you mention will not now even speak to me."

In Sargent's studio one day I remarked on the wonderful vitality of a portrait that was being sent home. "Yes," he said, "another enemy."

I have always admired the courage of Sargent, Sickert, Orpen, and John for the way they chose to please themselves in painting a portrait – and in doing so to please posterity. I, on the other hand, have too often tried to please the sitter, and like the man, the donkey, and the bridge, ended by pleasing nobody. I have felt ashamed of having spent my life trying to please sitters and make friends instead of telling the truth and making enemies.

So often it is a question of painting to please or not doing the picture at all. When I was in Seville I got one of the *gitano* girls from the tobacco factory to sit for me. I made a little dolled-up sketch first and gave it to her. She was delighted and would sit every day for the great picture I was to paint for myself. As the portrait progressed I found it difficult to work, as she kept coming behind me and throwing her arms round me, whispering, "*Muy bonito, muy brillante, muy precioso,*" and so on. But when I began to get a likeness and put some character into it she got furious, her eyes flashed, she tore the canvas off the easel, threw it on the ground, and rushed out – never to return.

Sometimes, when things have become desperate and foolish vanity has exceeded all bounds, I have found the candid camera useful to show sitters the truth and let them see what nature is really like in black and white. This, however, does not protect the painter from those who are anxious to get into the good graces of the sitter. "My dear" (if it is a woman), "he surely doesn't intend that for *you.* Why, he has made a fat old thing twice your age. Fortunately no one will recognize it. Don't let him exhibit it," and so forth. If it is a man's portrait: "My dear sir, I don't want to flatter you, but we all know you as a man of intellect and brilliant wit, not the senile wreck we see here. It is libelous and, in my opinion, actionable." All of which is swallowed neat. Of course, there are true friends who have no axe to grind and who support the painter, but unfortunately the true friend is not always listened to. Even many of the most intelligent people – including portrait painters themselves – resent *seeing themselves.* We all want beautiful pictures.

This is proved by the great difficulty the portrait painter has in doing a "speaking likeness" of himself. About thirty or more years ago I painted myself as a background for my little daughter – the picture liked by Whistler and now in the Luxembourg Gallery. After spending weeks painting the child and filling in the background, I left my own face until the last. I did it in one afternoon. It was considered a remarkable likeness. For I had not been bothering about myself. Shortly afterwards the Uffizi Gallery in Florence invited me to paint my portrait to be hung amongst the masters. Naturally I was anxious to hand down to posterity all my good qualities, and so I took two years over it, scraping out one attempt after another. Finally it was sent off, and my friends who saw it in the Gallery wrote and told me that I could not be as ordinary-looking as the man who comes to tune the piano or wind the clocks, that I had more distinction than I had given myself. I had no difficulty in believing them, so I wrote to the Director of the Gallery and made some excuse to get it back. After a couple of months I sent back the new version. There was no comment.

The other day I painted myself with Shirley Temple. Again it is said to be a speaking likeness. I was thinking of Shirley.

Most portrait and figure painters lean heavily on the camera while repudiating all connection with it – though their work becomes the strongest evidence to the contrary. There are exceptions such as Walter

Sickert, who publishes the source of his inspiration, and Linley Sambourne, who had the details of his work photographed before drawing them. Lenbach, the most distinguished German portraitist of our time, when he had sitters like Bismarck, the old Emperor, Von Moltke, and others who had little time for sitting, got over the difficulty by using the camera, and by concentrating on the head, especially the eyes, gave a vitality to his portrait work that no other portrait painter in Germany had reached.

Sargent gave up painting portraits for a time because, he said, he got tired of the sitter's "Now, Mr. Sargent, don't you think there is a little something about the mouth which is not just me?" It is a common fallacy to believe that the eye is the most revealing feature, or that the most striking features of a woman are her eyes and hair. As a matter of fact the most striking feature is her mouth. Mahomet knew this when he had his womenkind cover theirs up. The eyes can dissemble, but not the mouth. Every woman knows it to be her chief attraction, and to-day does her best with lipstick to add to her sex and increase her power to dissemble and disarm. A man cannot very well look into her eyes while they talk without a certain feeling of embarrassment, but he may concentrate his eye on her lips and believe that he is making progress without exposing himself. Lipstick is, to-day, widely used in the strict sense of the word; for a time women aimed at a little buttonhole of a mouth or a cupid's bow, but the movies have changed that to a large sensual gash, which is easy to paint and obscures the character in a way that is pleasing to the female and passes muster as a likeness for the painter.

Hair can be made to disguise features more than anything else, short of remodeling them. I remember painting Mrs. Brown Potter, who may not have been a very great actress but, by rearranging her masses of rich auburn hair, was able to make herself anything from an angel to a devil. Shortly afterwards, I was invited to paint a lady much talked of in Paris for her beauty and chic – Madame la Comtesse de Bec de Lièvre. She had what is called an Eton crop. I was terribly disappointed, for coming straight from Mrs. Brown Potter made me blind to the boyish beauty of the Parisienne.

Finally – a good example of trying to please everyone – a Lady Somebody wanted a semi-state portrait to hang beside the Gainsborough and Romney in the ancestral hall of her husband, who was to know nothing until the work was complete. The day at last arrived and with it the husband. Planting himself in front of the picture with both hands resting on a gold-headed cane, he maintained an ominous silence while his eyes roamed over the canvas. At last, raising a hand, covering the figure, and concentrating on the head, he spoke. "I pass the forehead and the eyes. I move my hand downwards: the nose, the mouth, the chin, them also I pass. I move my hand yet lower: what is this flat-chested modernity that I see? Where is the snowy amplitude of Her Ladyship? No, Sir John Lavery, that does not represent my wife." Her Ladyship stood by his chair almost in tears, saying, "I will not have an eighth of an inch added." I had tried to please both and, of course, had failed. Later I wrote to His Lordship that I felt he was justified in his criticism, and that if he was still in the same mind I would, with his permission, cancel the commission, and that he should take back the very expensive and highly carved frame he had ordered. He accepted.

I painted over the canvas another portrait, and the picture was irreverently but relevantly christened by a friend who knew both the originals – "Hail Mary, full of Grace."

XIV

SOME OF MY SITTERS

Mr. Hugh Spottiswoode came to me in 1912 with a commission to paint the Royal Family after the manner of Winterhalter's "Queen Victoria and Prince Albert," which, with their Majesties' permission, he proposed to present to the nation. The King and Queen were not in favor of the whole family, and suggested that the picture should only include the Prince of Wales and Princess Mary, besides themselves. The Queen expressed a wish to see my idea of the grouping, and a sketch I made was pronounced satisfactory, so I was permitted to have the White Drawing Room for a studio.

After the studies were made the picture was painted in my studio at Cromwell Place, where the King and Queen came to see the finished work. They were so pleased that the King said he would like to have a hand in it, and thinking that royal blue might be an appropriate color, I mixed it on the palette, and taking a brush he applied it to the Garter ribbon – the Queen, not to be outdone, following his example. It is recorded that when Velásquez completed "Las Meniñas," King Philip asked for a brush and color and painted the Red Cross of the Knights of Calatrava on the breast of the painter in the picture.

In 1934, when the Prince of Wales was sitting for the "Master Mariner" picture, he asked me many pertinent questions about painting in general. Then he said, "I am going to ask you an impertinent question, but you need not answer it. How much are you getting for the picture?" I told him. Putting his hand to his head, he exclaimed, "My God!" "Do you think, sir, I am charging Lord Wakefield too much or too little?" I asked. He smiled and said nothing. There were nearly a hundred portraits in the picture, for each of which I painted a separate study; and after the sitting I showed them to him. "Ah," he said, "I now understand." He had evidently thought my fee was too high.

Although he showed great patience while being painted, and recognized how necessary it was to give the painter every assistance, the Prince could not help remarking that, at the moment, he was doing the work of a professional model by sitting to at least five or six artists of different kinds, not including photographers, who were taking up every minute he could spare.

I had the same problem to solve in the "Master Mariner" picture that faced me in the "Surrender of the German Fleet" — that of mixing electric light and white fog. One light is inclined to obliterate the other, resulting in negation of effect, the subtlety of the color scheme being practically lost on the spectator. The other artificially lit scenes which I have painted, such as "The House of Lords" or "Wimborne House," have been frankly candlelight or electricity, and therefore much more obvious.

There is no greater charm than the mixture of the violet of twilight and the orange of electric or lamp light. But perhaps only Whistler has successfully got this on to canvas.

A large part of a portrait painter's life naturally consists of gazing upon the countenances of endless sitters. One must concentrate upon those faces, and it is only chance what one may remember concerning other things about them, or their wisecracks, if any. But I thought I might bring together into one chapter a few of those who sat for me, and I will do so right away, without regard to any chronological or other order.

BERNARD SHAW

It was somewhere back in the nineties that I first met G.B.S. I did not like the cut of his tightly buttoned Victorian jacket, its snuffy color, or his bilious tie — the latter more or less hidden by his beard. I could not see how I could paint his portrait and leave out his clothes unless I copied Rodin's "Victor Hugo" and painted him in the nude. Still, I very much wanted to paint him, so I tried a burberry coat, but it was a failure. He was very patient and allowed me to go on experimenting and showed no signs of boredom.

On another occasion, in 1911, when he was sitting for me, E. A. Walton wrote from Glasgow asking me if I could induce Shaw to sit for him. This is the reply I received: —

The frightful truth is that I am too completely out of date to know Walton's work. If he is a successful, fashionable painter my terms for thirty-two hours' sitting in eight acts are £2000 down in advance of a royalty of 15 per cent on the proceeds of the exhibition of the picture. If he is a man of genius tell him that I gave a month to Rodin and immortality, for the rest I shall be satisfied with photographs. Besides, I have promised about six painters — among them Rothenstein — my next sitting, bar the one I have just promised Madame Tussaud. G. B. S.

He was very devoted to Hazel, and when he came to sit for her I took advantage of it and painted him at the same time. Looking at both studies after a couple of hours, he addressed Hazel very deliberately: "Now, my dear, I think without doubt that yours is the worst portrait that has ever been done of me," — her eyes filled with tears, — "but I am coming back."

He came, and after sitting as long as she wanted he made up for his former harshness by expressing a desire that we should send the portraits to the Royal Academy. We did. As I was a member, mine was accepted, Hazel's rejected. Two Laverys and two Shaws were too much. But her work was much better than mine and was sold at once in the new Chenil Gallery, where she exhibited it. Mine was hawked round Europe and America, even to the extent of being shown at an exhibition in Tokio.

No one wanted it, so I destroyed it by painting another over it which now adorns the gallery of an American admirer of the great man.

I began a conversation piece hoping to get Charlotte in, as it was her house and the last days of Adelphi Terrace. Unfortunately she has strong objections to being painted, so G.B.S. appears alone, somewhat dejected, on a sofa.

I do not know whether it was the loneliness or the worry of removal that caused him to say that he had never known the comfort of a home until he moved into the modern flat in Whitehall Court that he now occupies. Of course he would say that. Anyway, the picture is now in the Modern Gallery at Dublin as part of the "Hazel Lavery Memorial Collection."

When Shaw had completed *Saint Joan*, doubts arose in his mind regárding the possibility of error in some of his statements of the Saint's faith. Since he was not a Catholic himself, and had been brought up in one of the protesting beliefs of his native city, Dublin, he thought it best to consult an expert on the question, Father Leonard, a lecturer at St. Mary's College, Hammersmith, who happened to be a friend of mine.

After writing the preface he showed it to the Father and asked, "Is it all right?" Father Leonard replied, "I think it's all wrong!" This was the beginning of a friendly controversy which ended by G.B.S.'s writing, "If this continues it will end by my becoming a Roman Catholic and you an agnostic."

SIR JAMES BARRIE

The three names I associate with the Adelphi are Shaw, Barrie, and Joseph Pennell. When the last-named died in America I cabled Mrs. Pennell the condolences of the International Society, stating that we wished to hold a memorial service. I knew she was a Catholic, and was very much surprised to find that her late husband was a Quaker, – the only belligerent one I have ever known, – and on making inquiries I found that the Friends did not hold memorial services; but there was a meeting place where silence and contemplation prevailed until a member of the body felt impelled to speak. I considered that some sort of public tribute should be paid him, and I telegraphed to Barrie and Shaw asking their presence at the Meetinghouse. Barrie replied with sympathy, accepting. Shaw's telegram simply read, "No John No Shaw."

Barrie often dined with us and we with him. He usually took us to Gatti's, in the Strand, where we would spend the evening talking. He enjoyed Hazel's company very much, although in his own home he preferred men. Like John Knox, he inveighed against "the monstrous regiment of women," saying that he had the greatest difficulty in keeping them out – "they get in through the cracks." This was when I was painting him. Shortly after I found that he had Lady Cynthia Asquith with him as private secretary, and a close friend in Lady Juliet Duff, with whom he seemed proud to be seen. Yet he was sensitive about his height, a little over five feet, and favored one portrait I did of him at work, writing on a hard wooden bench in his inglenook, with his knees drawn up supporting a little board with sheets of foolscap on which he wrote. The end of the bench was in semi-darkness, making it difficult to determine the height of the sitter.

I told him that since he liked the portrait I would bequeath it to the National Gallery of Scotland, and he wrote back: —

ADELPHI TERRACE HOUSE
20th October 1935

MY DEAR LAVERY, —

What you tell me makes me feel much beholden to you. I am very much complimented by your generosity and of course also by the National Gallery of Scotland's acceptance. It is certainly a charming picture, though no doubt some other head might be more interesting on the shoulders of the sitter. Don't you go and make use of that suggestion.

My warm thanks,
J. M. BARRIE

During the Treaty Negotiations, when Michael Collins was here on safe-conduct, canceling for a time the £10,000 reward on his head, I was astonished to find that he spent his odd moments, when not at the British Museum, Brompton Oratory, or my house, with Barrie. Physique allied with intelligence fascinated Barrie — hence he also was captivated by Gene Tunney, whose special favorites were Shakespeare and Bernard Shaw.

JOHN MASEFIELD

Recently I was asked to paint a picture of John Masefield, by an American admirer of his. I knew that he was a lover of the sea and that his hobby was making model boats, so I at once visualized his study as a miniature shipyard, and I was not far wrong, for it is practically that. His house is in the most beautiful part of the Cotswolds, overlooking undulating landscape of great beauty. The house dates from the sixteenth century and is of the Cotswold gray stone, an extensive rambling place made very comfortable by such modern devices as central heating and the like. Remembering the discomfort of country houses fifty years ago, I appreciated that.

The poet met me at the station eight miles from Pinbury Park, driving his own car, and set about loading my luggage; even one especially heavy box containing my painting equipment did not deter him, although his right hand is crippled with arthritis, which forces him to write with a typewriter and shake hands with his left. I spent with him some of the most pleasant weeks I can remember. From the moment I arrived until my departure, every desire was anticipated and attended to with an almost embarrassing consideration.

Masefield has a very natural antipathy to having his study invaded, and he keeps it barred against intruders. When I first suggested that I should like to paint him in it, his manner was so polite that I had no suspicion that I was proposing to make the Holy of Holies my studio.

When I discovered that he was having a new lock put on the door my courage for a moment failed me, for I realized that my *motif* was lost. Masefield saw that I was greatly disappointed, and a fellow feeling made him relent. From then on he put himself and the study at my disposal, and I have rarely had a more patient sitter. All the more patient, I may add, since I took a mean advantage of him by giving him some of this manuscript to read while I was painting him—so that he could not very well doze or skip.

SARAH BERNHARDT

Mrs. Patrick Campbell, the subject of a masterpiece by C. H. Shannon, had said in that deep rich voice of hers when I tried to paint her, "Ah, you do not paint me *con amore!*" and left me in the midst of it. But she wrote from Paris that she had been to the Salon with the "Divine Sarah," where they had seen a portrait of Lady Diana Manners. "The moment that Sarah saw it she said, 'The artist who painted that must paint me for my son. I like his point of view.' I told her that I knew you and that I would write and tell you. She wants to know your fee and if you could do it next month, when she is in London, or whether you would prefer to come to Paris."

I wrote to Mrs. Campbell that I should be delighted to paint her when she was in London, and that between artists there was no such thing as a fee. Sarah would not have that, so I mentioned a nominal sum. I got the most flattering letter in answer, saying that she would sit on condition that I would accept double the fee I first mentioned. I told a mutual friend in Paris, who was not so impressed by her generosity as I was. He said, "That's really mean of her; she ought to have said ten times what you are asking, as she never pays!"

When she came to London I was invited to her dressing room at the Coliseum. There she was, sitting in the fierce light of her make-up glass, the rest of the room in semidarkness. I could make out one or two people, among them a painter called Spendler who many years ago had painted a full-length portrait of her that she liked. She seemed to have hypnotized him and made him her painter-in-ordinary, as he had continued, I believe, painting her throughout the years. He came forward and introduced himself. Many years before, about the time that Bastien-Lepage had painted his famous profile portrait of her, I had seen her often on the Paris stage and was quite prepared for the hand of time; but not for the terrible havoc it had made of everything but her voice, which still had its old thrill and fascination. When she spoke one lost sight of the old withered woman with bare shoulders whose face in its stage make-up was fit for a surrealist. I was surprised that she allowed me to see her under such impossible conditions.

The first sitting was arranged for eleven o'clock the next morning and whenever she had no matinee. If that would not be enough, I was to come to Paris, stay with her, and use her studio. "Time does not count where a masterpiece is at stake," she said. There was an atmosphere of awe in the dressing room, everyone showing deference to the greatest tragedienne of the age.

Next morning she came looking very different from the night before, wrapped in furs – the most becoming of all frames to the face when age sets in. She had, in spite of everything, been given the most wonderful reception and was enthusiastic over "the great, enlightened English people who never forget." She was in high spirits and looked at least twenty years younger.

Remembering Spendler's portraits of her and how, after years, he has stuck to his first vision, and the fact that my commission had been brought about by a picture of Lady Diana Manners, I could see that fifty years would have to come off if I was to please. The whites of her eyes showed under the iris, particularly when she was looking upwards, giving a sentimental expression which I disliked and modified. She gave me a long sitting, two hours in all, posing like a professional and carrying on a most animated conversation with her friends. Spendler stood apart at a distance, making notes in a sketchbook, and when the sitting was over he shook me warmly by the hand, saying that for years he had not had such an opportunity. But she looked at what I had done, said, "*C'est pas mal!*" and never came back. I suppose the shock of seeing something so very different to the Diana picture which I had painted in a couple of hours was too much for her. She made some polite excuse, asking me to postpone the work for the moment. Possibly she may not have liked the painter, when she got to see more of him — an amusing instance of which I had on another occasion, when I painted Miss Walsh.

MISS WALSH

One morning I received a letter from the "Walsh Portrait Memorial Committee of Girton College" stating that they wished to have a portrait of the retiring Principal, and that she would call and arrange about sittings. She called one day when I was out, and was taken up to the studio and shown some portraits. The following day I had an express letter from the Secretary saying that the Committee had not yet definitely decided who was to paint the portrait. Meanwhile I had accepted an invitation to meet Miss Walsh at luncheon. I thought that if I went I would embarrass her, but if I did not go, it would look as if I were hurt at not getting the commission. I was sure she had not liked what she had seen in the studio. I went to lunch and she was extremely affable, asking me when I was going to begin the portrait. I explained that the Committee had not yet decided who was to paint it. She said that was all right, as the choice of the painter was in her hands, and when I got home I found another letter from the Committee confirming their commission.

The explanation came out afterwards. It seems that a sinister-looking man was leaving my house when she called. She said to the lady who came with her, "If that is the artist I saw going out, I couldn't be in the same room with him for five minutes."

To give the sitters something to occupy their minds I place a mirror so that they can see what is going on. This has a double advantage: they soon forget they are being looked at, and they get accustomed to the painting from the beginning and there is no shock at the end. Miss Walsh was very delicate and could not sit for long at a time, so I used to work on the portrait when she was away. Each morning she would take her seat in the chair, arrange herself, and then look at the reflected portrait in the glass. I would judge from her expression how she thought I was getting on with it. One morning, after going through her customary arrangement, when she looked in the mirror a strained expression in the eyes made me think I had not done so well. The look deepened to one of distress, and I was indeed feeling most anxious when, without rhyme or reason, she suddenly burst out laughing. The position of the looking glass had been changed, and she had been looking at herself. She was a charming Irishwoman with a keen sense of humor. When the portrait was being presented to the College she told of her two mistakes – "that the artist was another man and the portrait another woman; both great improvements on the originals!"

There is a curious perversity about things that happen to me time and again. In the case of Miss Walsh, when she walked into the studio that first morning, looking anything but like a picture from my point of view, and got into the "fierce light which beats upon a [model's] throne," I really felt helpless, and knowing that owing to her delicate state of health there would be no time for experimenting did not ease matters. I could see I was making her nervous, walking round and round her in a vain effort to see something that I could make into a design, and getting more stupid every moment. In desperation I had to do something or give up; that was the spirit in which I took up my brush to paint one of the best portraits I have ever done – or so I have been told, and I have no difficulty in believing it.

PAVLOVA AND LILY LANGTRY

Mr. Bruce Ingram, of the *Illustrated London News*, asked me to paint a portrait of Pavlova, giving me carte blanche. Having had some experience of painting actresses, and finding less trouble with Royal personages, I made conditions before agreeing to undertake the commission. I was to get a reasonable number of sittings, and some kind of undertaking that appointments would be kept. This was necessary, as most of the professionals I had painted in the old days behaved as if they were conferring a great favor by allowing themselves to be put on canvas, and acted accordingly. Before the telephone was in general use, and when my efforts as a portrait painter were not considered by my sitters as of supreme importance, I had many a bitter hour of frustration. Perhaps for days and nights, in some cases, I would be working out a design and pose for the proposed subject. By the time she was expected – men were usually less capricious – I would have worked myself to fever heat. The hour would arrive but not the sitter. By the evening or next day a telegram would come with some trivial excuse such as "Fog in our part of town," "At a dance last night, not looking my best this morning," or merely, "So sorry did not come to-day," and sometimes not even that.

Of course there were exceptions. Long ago I met Lily Langtry at a charity ball. She had come as a Bacchante and I as Rembrandt. It was thought that it might be an attraction, as well as a profit, if I painted her portrait, put it up for auction, and gave the proceeds to charity, which was done. In addition, a drawing appeared in the *Graphic* of "Rembrandt painting the Lily," which added to its value. Besides the freshness of her beauty I was greatly taken by her charm of manner. She made me feel I was one of the most interesting people she had met for years. That was in the eighties. A few years ago, in Monte Carlo, I met her again. She was with her maid in a tea shop. I did not recognize her, but Hazel did. She remembered me, or if she did not she made a perfect pretense, and she was genuinely glad to meet my wife. We talked of old times, of the late Victorian days and the short-lived Edwardian period. I told her of a dinner party I had been to, where the Georgians were "under the hammer" and a fashionable lady was heard to say, "Poor dears, they will never get into Society." A slight smile played about her still beautiful lips but she made no comment. She told us that she suffered so much from loneliness, as she had no one to talk to but her maid. She invited us to go to her villa, but when we telephoned a few days later she was too ill to see us; a week later she was dead.

Pavlova was another exception to the rule of discourtesy. I naturally expected the greatest dancer of all time to be a difficult problem, and that when it got into the papers that she was sitting, interviewers, photographers, souvenir hunters, and admirers by the hundred would besiege the studio. Cromwell Place would be lined with cars carrying dressers, electricians, and all the paraphernalia of the stage; and then, when everything was set, Pavlova would not appear, and if she did it would be to complain that she had no time, that she had a command performance, or something equally tiresome.

I was entirely wrong. She arrived unheralded and alone in a taxi, carrying her Bacchante dress tied up with a piece of pink ribbon. My wife's maid helped her to put it on. For a whole morning she posed, almost without resting, going through the "Dance Bacchanal" in slow motion that I might better see the position and the action, explaining that she was doing her regular and necessary exercises and that I must not think I was exhausting her. She came three or four times a week during her Palace engagement, and never once missed or was late for an appointment. Telegrams and letters came during the sitting, but she looked at none until the end. One day when she was posing on the floor for the Swan picture, now in the Tate Gallery, Monsieur d'Andrée brought in over a dozen large photographs to submit for her choice. It was the only occasion I saw her really displeased; she looked daggers at d'Andrée, asking what he meant, and so on, all in Russian, and, taking the photographs, she tore them into pieces one by one.

She refused all aids to comfort while posing, if she thought they would interfere with the aspect of the position I was painting. On the stage she had a look of Hazel. In "La Mort du Cygne," in Pavlova's dress, Hazel might have been taken for her with a little make-up. Seen together they were very different – the one dark, the other fair. Pavlova was large-boned and a trifle angular compared with the other. Close up, posing for the "Swan," Hazel appeared as Pavlova did in the distance on the stage. Sargent came into the studio when Hazel was posing and also remarked on the strange resemblance. He asked her to sit for one of his charcoal drawings, which she did some time afterwards and was delighted with the result. When she was looking in at it one day with Lytton Strachey, he remarked that there was always something sinister about Sargent's women. "But," she said, "he has only made me look sixteen." "That is what is so sinister about you," said Strachey, "and he has caught it."

RACING PICTURES

Steve Donoghue came to sit in the King's colors. I had just completed "Ascot in Rain" and asked him what he thought of it. The horses were nearing the post, and I expected him to criticize the drawing of the animals or the seats of the jockeys. Instead he began praising the picture: "It is beautiful – the most wonderful racing picture I have ever seen." "Now look here, Steve, I want to know what's the matter with it. Suppose you were talking with another jockey. What would you say?" After some hesitation he replied, "Well, I should say the visibility is too great." He was right. There was more detail than could be seen at the moment I had depicted. I brushed half of it away and, entirely owing to him, made a good picture.

No one could have been more considerate or helpful as a sitter. He arrived every morning punctually until the last sitting, when he was an hour late, explaining that he had had to "waste" a couple of pounds. "Can you do that in an hour?" "Easily," he replied. "Some healthy lady friends of mine would like your recipe." "Turkish baths and no drink." I asked him who was most reliable for a tip – the owner, the trainer, or the jockey. "I would say the trainer, if he knows the jockey."

One day in the weighing room at Epsom I told a jockey that if he would sit ten minutes in the scales he would win the next race. By sheer luck he came in first. I painted "13" on a saddlecloth in the picture. No. 13 was the next winner. After that each jockey as he went out touched me for luck. I overheard one say to an inquirer for a tip, "Ask the artist."

Lord Derby invited us down for the Autumn Meeting

at Newmarket. Hazel, who was new to race meetings in England, thought that I should be fittingly dressed for the occasion. She took me to Harrod's for a velours hat and a Newmarket coat. I was anxious to make a picture of the scene, and with my painting outfit was driven to a good viewpoint. I was setting up my things when a policeman came over, saying rather aggressively, "Have you got permission to be here?" "Yes." "Show it me." "I haven't got a written permission, but it is all right, I am staying with Lord Derby." "Oh, you are, are you? We've heard that story before. Pack up and look damned sharp." "You are making a mistake. Look, there is Lord Derby in the distance. You had better see him before you go any further." He thought it might be as well to interview His Lordship, so off he went. No sooner was he gone than his place was taken by a mounted policeman. "Now, young 'un, clear out." Feeling quite safe, I said authoritatively, "Who told you to speak to me like that?" "Orders from the Chief." "Now, you go back to the Chief and tell him I'm not a young 'un and I'm not going to clear out." For a moment he looked as though he would ride me down. The other policeman came running back, waving his arms and shouting, "It's all right, Bill." After that I could not see the course for police protection. It was the velours hat that caused the trouble – I had been mistaken for a bookie.

After my Newmarket experience I thought it might be as well to get properly accredited before attempting the Gold Cup at Ascot. I wrote to the Secretary and explained that I wanted to paint a general impression of the course. Orders came that I was free to choose any spot to paint from, so I chose a corner of the owner's stand where I had the best view. When I arrived I found the place railed off so that I could not be interfered with, so I put up my sketching umbrella and started work. I could not quite understand why every member when he arrived looked anything but pleased. Then I realized that I was in the Holy of Holies, usurping the spot reserved for the high and mighty; and not that alone – my umbrella was blocking the view. I took it down at once and made myself as small as possible just as the rain came down in sheets, pouring down my back and mixing with the paints. Having caused such consternation I had to stand it and two weeks in bed afterwards.

I was asked to paint for Doncaster an official portrait of Lord Lonsdale in Garter robes, but I could not imagine him without a cigar and tweeds. To me he was the most paintable – not to say the best-dressed – Englishman I knew. To help matters I introduced his yellow coach, complete with powdered lackeys, but it did not do him justice, although he would not admit it. When I pressed him for a criticism he only remarked that he thought the yellow of the coach was more effective in the gray of London than in the green of the country. I was determined to do a more typical picture of him in his everyday clothes. The result was, I think, more successful.

STATESMEN

In pre-War days a week end in the country meant Friday to Tuesday. That never suited me – a strange bed meant no sleep. When the War came there was less time to spare, and a run in the country for lunch or dinner on a Sunday had to suffice statesmen, generals, and the rest for relaxation.

One such Sunday at Lady Paget's, at Kingston Hill, Winston Churchill and I were painting with no one taking much notice of us, when a hale-and-hearty voice behind called out, "Hello, Winston, when did you begin this game?" Without turning round Winston replied, "The day you kicked me out of the Admiralty, Lord Charles." "Well," said Beresford, "who knows? I may have saved a great Master."

Mr. Churchill has been called a pupil of mine, which is highly flattering, for I know few amateur wielders of the brush with a keener sense of light and color, or a surer grasp of essentials. I am able to prove this from experience. We have often stood up to the same *motif*, and in spite of my trained eye and knowledge of possible difficulties, he, with his characteristic fearlessness and freedom from convention, has time and again shown me how I should do things. Had he chosen painting instead of statesmanship I believe he would have been a great master with the brush, and as P.R.A. would have given a stimulus to the art world.

Winston enjoyed bicycling, and during one of these

week ends Eddie Marsh went out with his chief. On his return he was asked how they had got on. He answered, "Winston rode, I ran."

As I have already said, my interest in politics is nil, although I did allow myself to express a decided opinion on the Irish situation in a letter from Armagh, but this did not exclude me from making friends with some statesmen. Amongst these I think Mr. Lloyd George has pride of place. Not because he settled the Irish Question (more or less), won the War, gave me a knighthood, and, it is said, "bitched the peace," but because of his great charm. I do not know who wrote the following lines, whether I quote correctly or even if they are copyright, but they are too entertaining to be overlooked, and I feel sure that no one enjoys them more than the subject: —

> Lloyd George no doubt, when his life pegs out,
> Will ride in a fiery chariot,
> And sit in state on a red-hot plate
> 'Twixt the devil and Judas Iscariot.
> Ananias that day to Satan will say,
> "My claim to precedence now fails.
> Please move me up higher, away from the fire,
> And make room for that liar from Wales."

It was of the utmost importance that a picture of him should be included in the Dublin collection, and whenever there was a chance of a sitting I rang up his private secretary. But he was an exception to the rule that the more a man does the more easy it is for him to find time. It was not until he got settled at Churt that I finally tracked him down, to find him the most amenable of sitters. At that time he was working on his War memoirs, so I painted him writing in his study. I thus had the double advantage of catching him in a characteristic pose and not feeling that I was encroaching too much on his time.

Although only an amateur farmer he carried off most of the prizes at local shows, and when congratulated expressed the belief that his success was due to the fact that he was supplied with manure from the cavalry barracks at Aldershot: "Perhaps the greatest benefit I have received from the Government."

I painted Mr. Asquith's portrait for the National Liberal Club with the help of "Margot," to whom I am truly indebted. I was most anxious to paint the scene in the Cabinet at midnight on August 3, 1914, with the Members waiting for the declaration of War. He was very nice about it, and to my numerous questions quite sympathetic. When I pressed him for further details he said, with no sign of rudeness but excusing his want of memory, "I must have been thinking of something else." He was an excellent sitter and kept me amused with reminiscences. He said he enjoyed his years at the Bar but considered that brilliant repartee was dying out there just as it was dying out of conversation. He gave me a good example of Tim Healy's wit, which I had not heard before. Someone had spoken of the girl in the dock as being "pure as the driven snow." "Oh, I see," flashed Healy, "a hoar frost."

My first meeting with Margot Asquith was some time in the nineties. I was walking down West George Street, in Glasgow, with the Master of the Renfrewshire Hounds, when a hansom cab drew up suddenly in front of us and a beautiful girl, dressed in the height of fashion, waved wildly to him. He rushed forward and assisted her to alight, introducing her to me as Miss Tennant. In the dull gray of the Glasgow streets this very vital creature took my breath away. I had heard of her as the most fearless rider to hounds in the country, and now I had met her, this was easy to believe. She will have forgotten that meeting, as I have very good reason to know. Thirty years passed, and it was at No. 10 Downing Street that she came to me after dinner, saying, "Come into the other room, I want to show you my Lavery." It was a portrait by Laszlo.

If we except American women, there are few who know more about dress or how to decorate themselves to the best advantage than Lady Oxford. In the many years I have known her I have only once felt inclined to question her taste, and that was one morning when she came to sit in skiing clothes. But then I dislike women in trousers, even in riding breeches; some of them like to look masculine, but there is no more unbecoming garment worn by women.

I remember Margot of the heart of gold and free tongue standing in front of a picture of mine in the Royal Academy. "What's this? Fish, flesh, or fowl? Mostly foul." Hazel could not bear to have my work ridiculed and I doubt if she ever really forgave her, but she never missed an opportunity of going to The Wharf when we were invited. She admired Lord Oxford, and enjoyed nothing so much as being taken round the colleges and meeting the dons. I, of course, stayed behind making pictures of that lovely backwater at Sutton Courtenay. In spite of such criticisms Lady Oxford is kindness itself and has a really keen sense of the points of a picture. I have often thought what a perfect model she would be for "Good Queen Bess," with her clear bright eyes, aquiline nose, thin lips, and pointed chin.

It was at one of her Downing Street parties that I was presented to a dear old lady, — I often see age in people years younger than myself, — Countess Benckendorff, the Russian Ambassadress. We became great friends, and afterwards on such occasions she invariably made for me when the men joined the ladies after dinner. Putting her arm through mine, she would say, "Now, Mr. Lavery, we shall sleep togezzer on the sofa!" Going out at night was exhausting after struggling all day with portraits, so it was a great relief not to have to make conversation, and no doubt she felt the same.

Lord Birkenhead and Sir Patrick Ford were the first to suggest that I should paint their separate Houses. Hitherto nobody had ever been permitted to set up an easel in either House while Parliament was in session, but Sir Patrick knew that I was able to work under any conditions, and introduced me to the Sergeant-at-Arms, explaining my mode of procedure. Eventually all objections were overcome and I was allowed to take my pochade paintbox into the Distinguished Visitors' enclosure, where I was able to paint in comfort without my presence being known. From there I could see the whole House spread before me, including the Press and Ladies' Galleries. It turned out to be a much easier problem than I had anticipated. Since each Member had his allotted seat, which he retained long enough to feel at home there, I had plenty of opportunities of observing and choosing his favorite position. If I did not catch it at once I could feel that there would be other times when he would take up the pose again, which in many cases was quite unconscious. Besides studies of individual Members, I made one or two of the general scene with the Prime Minister, the Right Honorable James Ramsay MacDonald, addressing the House, surrounded by the members of the first Labour Government and the Opposition.

It was altogether a very pleasant experience, and after work I used to be entertained at dinner with Hazel in the Harcourt Rooms by Pat Ford. Then we would sit in the twilight on the Terrace and meet in friendly after-dinner chat both sides of the House. But my interest was always centred on the scene — the Members and their friends, many of the ladies in evening dress, walking in the subdued golden light up and down the long Terrace, against a background of the deep violet haze of the river, with the barges silently gliding past. The long row of buildings on the opposite bank reminded me of Whistler's "Palaces in the Night."

One night Hazel's attention was riveted by a man who stood apart with his arms resting on the parapet looking at the river. He certainly stood out amongst everyone there, and when he turned his sallow face in our direction, even in the half-light I could see the sparkling intensity of his green eyes. Sir Patrick saw that we were attracted, and said, "You are looking at one of the finest men in the House. That is James Maxton, the Member for Camlachie, in Glasgow." From that moment he became a great friend of Hazel's and one of my most picturesque sitters. He liked playing golf with me because, he said, I was the only man he could beat, but I think this was too modest an estimate of his game. I remember our first game at Ranelagh. He called for me in his little ramshackle two-seater, dressed in sports clothes that made his appearance even more striking; he looked as though he were one of a Glasgow crowd dressed for a "futaboll match on a Saturday." There were a number of members waiting their turn at the first tee, and they looked askance at my companion and me as we came up. The few who did recognize him disapproved strongly of his political views, but when he played off and landed his ball on the first green – a shot a professional might well be proud of – they unbent slightly.

Maxton told me a good golfing story. He was playing on the Barrhead course near Glasgow with the local "Meenister." A brook crosses the links, and every time the Meenister cleared it he would remark with grim satisfaction, "Once more over the bonnie wee burn"; but when he got into it he would mutter to himself, "Into that bloody sewer again." My golf has never been particularly good. I once told a Scottish caddie that I was not much of a golfer, and he agreed with me. To the same confession an Irish caddie replied, "Ah, sir, there are very few can play like you."

A little while ago a famous statesman was in my studio. Seeing Maxton's portrait, he said, "Ah, one of the few gentlemen left in the House."

I had a deep affection for Ramsay MacDonald because, by declaring himself a pacifist, he did the most courageous thing a man could do when the world was at war and when men, blinded by rage and hatred, were murdering each other, backed up by the churches in the name of patriotism and the sanctity of the home. He wanted to save his fellow men from what he considered one of the greatest blunders of history.

Hazel and I went to Scotland to paint him in his home, a house of four or five rooms in the village street of Lossiemouth. The kitchen was the main living room, and there I painted a group of the Prime Minister, his daughter Ishbel, and his housekeeper Jeannie, who had been at school with him. The place was filled with pressmen anxious for any news that might be obtained, and it got to be known that Jeannie was to be in the picture. One day she was laying the table for tea, the position she occupied in the picture, when one of the secretaries entered the room and said, "There's a man from London sent by a newspaper to interview you about this painting." "Aye, weel, you can juist gang awa' back and tell him A'm not going to say to folks like him what's passing between Sir John and me." The picture was progressing when I ran short of oil. I tried the chemist, who told me that there was a local artist who might oblige me. He turned out to be a water-color painter, but was able to root out some oil and showed me some excellent snow scenes he had done. Thinking to do him a good turn on the way back, I mentioned to a friend that I was going to ask the Prime Minister to dispose of the picture for him. "You had better not mention that artist's name to Ramsay. It was he who headed the group to burn down The Hillocks and, besides, had him expelled from the golf club." The first thing I was asked when I got back to work was, "Well, did you get the oil?" Forgetting what I had been told, I replied, "Oh yes, from the village painter." Ramsay at once said, "I had a letter from that man the other day asking me to let bygones be bygones; saying that times had changed and he hoped I would forgive. I replied that he should not be in a hurry, there was still plenty of time to change back again."

On the morning of his last public appearance he gave me a sitting for the unfinished portrait. We had luncheon together, and he said, "Well, John, I fear I may not manage to come back to you again; this afternoon I address the Royal Society, to be misunderstood as usual. Good-bye, and God bless you."

A week afterwards, on his way to South America to seek rest, he died.

Cunninghame Graham was most anxious to have me paint Parnell, and asked me to meet him in the House of Commons. Mr. Parnell was very gracious when Graham told him that I was the most distinguished Irish artist living (?), and after asking me one or two pertinent questions promised to come to the studio. But I never saw him again, for on the very day he was coming to sit he was what the Americans call double-crossed by Gladstone, of whom it was said by Michael Davitt, "Why, he is just an old ass spoiled by flattery," or, as Disraeli put it in more cultured language, "intoxicated by the exuberance of his own verbosity" – a very common failing amongst politicians.

But from that brief close-up of the great leader I could see and feel the power he exercised over his forces, and the truth of the many tales I had been told. There is one in particular that I recall. The debate was to be carried on until midnight, and Parnell was in the lobby walking up and down when suddenly he stopped and asked that the Member for —— should be sent to him. A minute or so later a disheveled, breathless man appeared and the following conversation took place. Parnell, looking at his watch, said in a clear sharp voice: –

"You are to speak for one hour from eleven o'clock."

"Sure, sir, I have nothing to say, and besides I don't know what they are after at all."

"What are you?"

"A farmer."

"Then talk about butter."

And he did, with such effect that there was a leader in *The Times* next morning congratulating the Irish Party on having at least one member with common sense and of some use to his country. "There is no doubt that his words, in bringing before us the great value of agricultural produce, give us food for thought which our own farmers would do well to profit by," and so on.

When I painted the House of Lords I was permitted to work in the Press Gallery looking down on their Lordships, not on a level with them as in the House of Commons. Unfortunately I was not near the Ladies' Gallery on the afternoon when two peers, both masters of invective, were engaged in trouncing each other over the Irish Question as it approached the solution. They were attentively listened to by their wives. One, losing her temper, kept repeating to herself in a voice the other could not fail to hear, "The dirty dog, the dirty dog!" At last the other replied, "Please change the sex of the animal and apply it to yourself."

The gentlemen of the Press were most considerate in pointing out some of the peers I did not know by sight. There was one I knew well – Lord Birkenhead. I had painted him in tweeds for the Inner Temple, besides dining with him on several occasions. He sits in state on the woolsack in the middle of the picture, with Lord Morley on his left, moving the address on the Irish Treaty to a full House.

When the picture was completed and on exhibition at the Royal Academy there was talk of purchasing it for the House of Lords, but it turned out to be only talk. I thought that it really ought not to be separated from the House of Commons picture, which had been purchased by the Corporation of Glasgow, so I made a gift of it to that city, and the two now hang side by side in the Kelvingrove Museum.

I first met F.E. at Grosvenor House when it was still the home of Gainsborough's "Blue Boy" and "Mrs. Siddons as the Tragic Muse," by Reynolds. Dinner was over, the ladies had left the table, and, conversation becoming general, the pros and cons of a recent case of blackmail were being discussed. It was in the days when there was considerable difficulty in suppressing the name of the victim. F.E., who was opposite me, suddenly said, "By the way, Lavery, I am very glad to have met you. I think I can be of service to you and your beautiful wife." I had at once an uncomfortable feeling that I was going to hear something very unpleasant. Truth to tell, I was frightened out of my wits. Not that I had a guilty conscience, but to be addressed like this by one of the most famous advocates of his time meant something sinister. "Yes," he said, "I think I can put ten thousand into your pocket." Conversation stopped and all eyes were turned on me. "Until now," he continued, "you who are most interested may have had no hint of the scandal identified with your good name. A story is going the rounds that no lady is safe in your studio, and a certain newly wed of a somewhat wayward nature went to your studio for her portrait. Finding her flirtatious, without more ado you locked the door. But she – young Amazon that she was – did not see things quite in that light and proceeded to teach you a lesson by tying your hands behind your back and leaving you helpless on the floor. She locked the door and returned with her husband, and the reason that you have not been seen about lately was because of his visit." Then I caught him winking at Bend'or, our host; that "blew the gaff" and relieved my blood pressure, which had been mounting during the story.

He had a weakness for showing off his alert mind. He was sitting next to the Prince of Wales one night at a public dinner where a speaker droned on and on beyond endurance. The prince, turning to F.E., said, "I wish to God that man would stop." "That's all right, sir," said F.E., and calling the toastmaster he wrote a card to be slipped at once to the speaker. The result was instantaneous. The speaker sat down. F.E. had written, "Adjust your dress."

Lord Darling, who was then Mr. Justice Darling, invited me to have lunch at the Old Bailey. I sat on the Bench and heard a criminal case being tried. When we retired with the judge for lunch I noticed a folded square of black cloth he placed on the table before disrobing. It was the Black Cap, of a shape worn by Erasmus in the Holbein picture. Up till then I had imagined it to be a kind of skullcap; in reality it is quite loose, and when the dread moment comes the Clerk of the Court stands behind the judge and places it over the wig. I was surprised that he should have it with him in the very ordinary case we had just heard, but he explained that in criminal cases at the Old Bailey the cap was always at hand.

He was much interested in art and agreed to let me paint him delivering the death sentence, of which he gave us an example then and there, but he made a proviso that I should not show the picture in England. Then, after he had thought a moment, he said, "You may show it in the Royal Academy if you will dedicate it to the Hanging Committee." He knew they had refused my work on more than one occasion. The picture eventually went to the New Salon, and when it came back I presented it to the Inner Temple. F.E. thought the subject unfitted for pictorial treatment and in the worst possible taste. He was still more upset when Darling asked me to make a picture of the Roger Casement Appeal, at the Central Criminal Court, promising to give every possible help. I had the use of the jury box, from where everything was to be seen stretched out before me — the five judges, the prisoner behind bars in the dock with hard-faced warders on either side, the array of counsel, and as many of the public as the court could hold. I managed to keep my paintbox out of sight, but the prisoner suspected, in fact he knew, because he wrote from the condemned cell, as I learnt from his sister, Mrs. Parry: —

OXMEAD, EWHURST
SURREY
Dec. 2nd, 1916

DEAR MR. LAVERY, –

In the letter to me, written on the 18th July, from Pentonville, in which Roger makes a very witty survey of the proceedings in the Court of Criminal Appeal, he writes, "Who was the painter in the jury-box painting a picture of the court? I should think he came dangerously near 'aiding and comforting' if not indeed 'compassing' from the way he eyed Mr. Justice Darling delivering judgment. Surely it is treason to take a Judge's head off on the Bench!" Later in the same letter he asked about your wife. I have copied out the passage for her.

I am sending you a copy of the photograph I showed you. I had a certain number done on big mounts, but they are all much lighter prints than this postcard and consequently not such good photographs. His eyes were a Spanish gray, which in some lights looked blue.

I am so grateful to you for allowing me to see your work, and I cannot be too grateful that it is an Irishman who is painting the picture.

With kind regards,
Yours sincerely,
GERTRUDE PARRY

To Hazel she wrote: –

I copy out for you the reference to you in the letter written July 18th in Pentonville by Roger:

"Who was the lady who sat near the painter in the jury-box? She was there yesterday too – to-day she came in late

— I thought I knew her face. It was very sad — and I kept on trying to remember. She had a wonderful face. I saw it all the time to-day."

When I saw him the day after he had written he asked me again about you and said, "Have you found out who the beautiful lady was? I wonder if she came with Beresford."

It was difficult to realize that a man's life was at stake in the drowsy monotony of the talk that went on for two days, or even at the end when Justice Darling, in the most casual manner, said, "The Appeal is dismissed." Casement stood up and looked round the court, waved to someone in the gallery, turned his back, and disappeared down the stairs that would finally lead to the scaffold.

XV

EXHIBITIONS

I THINK every art student starts with the belief that when he has gained a knowledge of the language he will be able to say something that has not been said before. In the majority of cases, as he goes on he finds that what he has to say has been said by somebody else, perhaps in language he can never aspire to. If he is a wise man he turns his training to account by becoming a teacher, provided he has the power to impart what he has acquired; a critic, if he can express himself in words; a curator of a gallery or a dealer, if he has business capacity. Then it will be seen that his time has not been wasted and he will at least be justified in what he takes up, which cannot be said of all the gentlemen engaged in these pursuits. As Sir Walter Raleigh says, in a letter quoted earlier in this book, "You can't understand an art you don't practise – never." Of course it must be admitted there are some rare beings who are born with an instinct that takes the place of acquired knowledge.

I have always thought it wiser to let the art critic have his say undisturbed, feeling that as an amateur writer I should have no chance against a professional. Even Whistler, when it came to a trial, was only awarded a farthing damages. Artists are apt to forget the position of the art critic who writes for the public and has to supply his journal – in many cases every day – with readable matter. How can he possibly have anything new to write about a painter with whom he is not in sympathy or on whose work he has written again and again? Of course there is the critic whose real interest is a literary one; he uses painting as a peg on which to hang an essay. What the artist really values is the opinion of the painter who does the job as well as if not better than himself; then he hears something he can ponder over.

I have sat on many juries at home and abroad, and if there is a more thankless task I have yet to hear of it. From all sides and in every conceivable way you are made to suffer for the vanity of the would-be exhibitor. Each and every one expects his or her work to occupy the most prominent place in the exhibition; not that alone, but it must not be interfered with by the color, design, or size of the neighboring pictures. I know that I have not done my fair share of this thankless task in the Royal Academy, partly owing to the fact that I was not in my first youth when I was elected and also because my health could not stand the strain of trying to be fair. Imagine judging the merits of, say, ten thousand pictures in a week, and the state of the eye and brain at the end of it. It is humanly impossible for me to be really just or impartial under those circumstances. In Ireland they speak of being "horse-blind." On selection committees I become "picture-blind."

It is hard on the portrait painter who is not a member of the Royal Academy to have to submit his work to the jury and have it rejected. In nine cases out of ten a portrait is of more interest to the subject and his or her friends than to the general public, so that when it comes before the selecting committee it has, perhaps, less chance of acceptance than other subjects — unless it is outstandingly good. The landscape and *genre* painters who send their work on sale resent wall space being taken up by commissioned portraits, although the gain to a landscape by contrast when placed by a portrait is enormous.

In Venice, where, I believe, the first exhibition of contemporary international art was held, it was thought that one important difficulty had been surmounted. The Italians were to judge foreign works and the foreigners Italian. One thing we foreigners forgot — the Italian artist was not accustomed to have his work submitted to a jury and resented rejection in a way that was not altogether pleasant. In fact, one artist blew out his brains when his work was refused. The feeling ran so high that the jury was advised not to be seen together and on no account to visit the Café Florian on the Piazza San Marco. The Italians were very considerate of our work, but not so of their own. The Florentines, the Romans, the Neapolitans, the Milanese, and the Venetians showed scant regard for each other. It came to a head when Antonio Fradeletto, who had made it possible for Italian artists to show their work in a public gallery in their own country, was accused of being *Austrian*. I thought there would be bloodshed, but we managed to calm them down before any damage was done.

It was at this time that I met one of the most brilliant and amusing men I have ever known – Ugo Ojetti, the distinguished writer and art critic. He made me realize what Antonio Fradeletto and his son Giuliano were doing for art in Italy, the extent of which few realized at the time. For myself, it is to them and to Ojetti that I owe my first outstanding successes on the Continent, and it was through them that I was invited to hold a large one-man show in Venice, in 1910, and five of my pictures were bought for public galleries in Rome and Venice.

The work that Fradeletto did in Italy was carried on in Germany by Adolf Paulus, who spent his life in combating the effete art that prevailed there at the end of the last century and brought about the first Secession at Munich and a far-reaching revival. Yet later he was deposed, without a word of thanks for his pains, and, like Fradeletto, is to-day forgotten.

XVI

HAZEL

My life has been largely a question of painting in my various studios – for the last forty years at Cromwell Place. Yet Cromwell Place, for many years, achieved another status: it was the meeting ground of a large number of famous people holding all sorts of views and engaged in many different activities.

These people did not come to see me. They came to see Hazel. She loved making friends, she had the gift, and the power to use it delighted her always. She enjoyed all sorts and conditions of people, and she was almost childishly anxious to win each and every one's esteem and affection. She was genuinely interested in all she met, old or young, celebrities or nobodies; to her they were somebodies because they were human beings and all humanity enthralled her – she was in love with the spectacle of life.

When illness took her hand from the pulse of the lives of others, she died. My life was my work – painting; her life was life itself.

She had much Irish blood, but she was primarily an American. An American of a particular type. An American aristocrat. I shall not be misunderstood when I say that Americans on the whole are still so vital, so young, so eager, that aristocracy – which is a late flower in a nation's life – is hardly yet developed in their great country. On the whole American women have other qualities, unique and fascinating. But there are some aristocrats already, doubtless prophetic of the future, in that favored land which flows with so much promise and holds up so much hope. They are to be met with here and there – in an office, behind a counter, in the home. They are amazingly different from the others. Sometimes they are active, as in the case of Amelia Earhart, whose simplest movement was informed with a kind of rugged royalty, but more often they have a sort of dreamlike quality about them in striking contrast to the make-it-snappy atmosphere of the country. They even build up something of an imaginary world and dwell in it. They possess a quality which can only be described by an out-of-date word in the Old World – goodness. Their eyes are large and have a certain age-old gaze about them that makes one think that these women belong to the most ancient rather than the youngest of nations.

Hazel was of this kind – though perhaps such eyes have not been seen elsewhere. She possessed that easy poise which conveys the suggestion neither of superiority nor of inferiority, but of equality with all. She was incapable of condescension and incapable of kowtowing. When equality is an ideal with people they either live up to it or down to it with an obvious effort. With Hazel it was not an ideal, but her natural feeling. Hence when she met Royalty there was no strain, for her manner was so naturally charming — and the King and Queen felt this, I think. Even her daughter Alice, at the age of five, showed it when she tried to interest the Queen by saying, "I have the same dancing mistress as your little girl." This freedom from embarrassment seemed a relief to Royalty, so accustomed to the not-speaking-till-spoken-to conventions. Americans have more right, I think, than any other republic to use the terms Liberty, Equality, and Fraternity.

Hazel loved to meet people who excelled in anything, and she was equally interested whether they were rulers, writers, soldiers, or painters. She herself, as I have pointed out before, was a very good artist, and her views on books were found so worth while even by Bernard Shaw that he used to send her batches of his *Intelligent Woman's Guide to Socialism* while he was writing it. But it was as a hostess that she excelled and found her true art. She had exquisite tact and discrimination, and mixed her friends with the ease and grace of the most successful diplomat. When they came, whoever they were, they all felt that they had something in common — this pleasure of the moment. All were made to feel at home, not just to feel they were being made to feel at home. And when they left the house they did not feel that they were being discussed unfavorably and pulled to pieces. They knew that Hazel did not do that, and that no one else did it in her presence.

Therefore she came to have a host, a regiment, of friends and admirers — and they numbered as many women as men. Not so many women at first; but as the years passed and no scandal could be fastened on her in any way at any time, her women admirers — especially the married ones — increased and became more and more amicably disposed towards her.

I do not know how many sitters, and wealthy ones, came to me on her account. For apart from these social gifts she made sitters talk to her, which set them at their ease while I was painting them. Lord Northcliffe, like Lord Lonsdale, loved to have her to talk to during the sittings. When they were over, the former, in the most charming manner conceivable, handed her a large check, saying, "My dear lady, you have revolutionized sittings." She was a little embarrassed, but he was so obviously sincere that she could only say "Thank you."

Any attempt to single out names and recall on this page the friendly faces that honored our house must be seen as impossible. Hazel left behind a trunkful of letters and mementos of those days. It is not for me to disturb them.

I have painted her portrait so many times. I have tried to do a sketch in words here because when I come to speak of Ireland, as I must now do, and mention the Treaty of 1921, Hazel's influence during the negotiations may not seem too fantastic to the reader.

But neither in paint nor in words do I feel I could ever

do justice to Hazel. Her rare beauty of face and character must have been known personally to be believed, and so upon the things nearest to me I will write least. We had twenty-five years together. She died in 1935, after a long illness.

XVII

IRELAND AND THE TREATY

"BREATHES there the man, with soul so dead," and so on. Well, shame to say, I am that man and still breathing, and what is still worse, I have known other lands that I like better than Ireland — at any rate for the time being. No country holds a monopoly of all virtues.

Sometime in 1879, when I was back in Glasgow, a Captain Beddoes, R.N., walked into my studio saying that he would like lessons in painting, and would I be his guest in Ireland, as he was stationed at Belmullet, County Mayo. I accepted the invitation, and his wife, a plump Englishwoman, gladly received me, telling me of the joy it was to her husband to have "a real artist" in the house.

I did not realize the difficulty of getting there, or I might have thought twice about the invitation. The railway ended at Ballina, and I had to hire a jaunting car for the thirty or forty miles to Belmullet, the driver on one side of the vehicle and I on the other, the luggage in the middle. Sitting back in our seats, we tilted up the car to such an extent that I was afraid we should lift the horse off its feet. If "jolting" were substituted for "jaunting" it would have been an admirable description of the vehicle.

The country was desolate. I'm afraid I'm too Irish to appreciate what a friend of mine calls "the poetry of desolation that is not abominable." I asked him where he felt desolate. "In the new suburbs of London," he said. "But things have to be new from time to time," I pointed out. He admitted that, and had no ready reply. After thinking for a long time as if trying to puzzle out his own point of view, he said that there was something wrong about the newness of the suburbs of London. "That does not take us very far," I ventured to reply. "They lack joy," he said. I reminded him that County Mayo could hardly be described as joyous. "It doesn't need to be," he said; "but if there is no joy in a new thing it is awful, and it chills the heart as no bog or desert can ever do. That is what is wrong with the new houses," he continued; "they are not made by singing masons building roofs of gold. That spirit is utterly unknown in modern England, hence its vileness and sin. . . ." My friend began to work himself up.

However that may be (as inconclusive people say) I did not get much kick out of that drive. We jogged along monotonously for an hour, the driver making vain efforts to interest me by telling me how wonderful the English are. After a while we stopped opposite a miserable thatched cottage; fishing a green apple out of his pocket, the driver offered it to me, saying that "it would keep down the drought." As it was getting bitterly cold I said I should prefer a hot cup of tea. "Tay, is it!" he said. "Sure, you couldn't drink the stuff they have in there!"

I took the hint and gave him a shilling. Handing me the reins, he was in and out of the cottage in a shot, bearing a bowl in one hand and wiping his mouth with the other. I tasted the "potheen" but preferred the winter apple. I cannot remember passing any other house on the road; it was all cold and dreary, making the Beddoes's house seem the acme of comfort.

One morning I was in the kitchen when a very good-looking girl brought in some eggs. She was certainly lovely, with a wild look in her eyes. Mrs. Beddoes, peering into the basket she put on the table, said, "I'm afraid, Norah, you are in the habit of taking the large eggs to Mrs. O'Grane and bringing the small ones here." The girl blushed with indignation, said not a word, lifted the basket and went out, never to return, though Mrs. Beddoes was her only other customer.

The poverty was terrible and on a par with that of Morocco. I wandered about the desolate place looking for something to paint, and on the lonely highroad I met a tall, upright, emaciated peasant woman striding along, a red shawl round her head. When I stopped her she looked terribly frightened, wondering what I could be after, laden as I was with painting things. I asked her if she would let me paint her, showing my brushes and canvas, but she did not understand English and shook her head. A barelegged, ragged creature came running down the road and joined her. They talked in Irish, and the boy, a sharp little lad, explained what was wanted. They stood watching me put up the easel and begin sketching, and after a time the boy came round to see what I was doing, but she remained where she was, her anxious eyes following every movement. She was sure there was something evil going on and began to edge away, until the boy called to her and she stood stock-still. I went on working and she seemed hypnotized. Feeling a bit nervous, I signed to her in a friendly way to come and look. She did not move, but remained rooted to the ground. Finishing off, I gave her a two-shilling piece and the boy some coppers. She kept turning the money over in her hands as if it were a foreign coin, – as in point of fact it was to her, – and finally, showing it to the boy, she walked away.

When I was painting in the North I asked Shane Leslie to give me some details of the famous place of pilgrimage, Saint Patrick's Purgatory, with the idea of going there myself and painting the scene. He wrote me an account which I cannot do better than quote here: –

In the Southern Highlands of County Donegal lies a lake – Lough Derg – some eleven miles around, circled by low, barren, heathery hills and studded with islands planted with trees. In the midst of the lake is the famous "Purgatory of Saint Patrick," as it is marked on all mediaeval maps. For centuries this has been a pilgrimage place of the Irish people.

According to the legend of Ossianic times a dragon was slain in the lake by the Fenian heroes under Finn MacCoul. The blood of the monster tinctured the lake and gave it its Gaelic name, Lough Derg. Saint Patrick took the place of the Druids with his anchorites, while he made their cave into a place of penance, promising that whoever remained penitently fasting therein should obtain remission of sins. In mediaeval times great sinners and desperate criminals arrived from all parts of Europe, failing of absolution in their own countries. If they survived the journey by the sea and by land they entered the cave in which they were locked by the Prior of the Purgatory, and remained there ten nights. If they survived this terrible ordeal they were accounted absolved from their sins and returned to live a new life. A number of them left remarkable accounts of what befell them in the cave, and the early glimpses which foretold some of the terrors of the next world are thought to have inspired Dante himself.

The Priory and the Purgatory were destroyed at the time of the Reformation and the place lay derelict. It passed under the jurisdiction of the Bishops of Clogher and later became part of the property of the Leslies of Glaslough. During the nineteenth century there was an astounding lawsuit between the landlords and the bishops. When it came before the courts as a dispute for the Fee Simple of the ground of the Purgatory, it was found that the English law recognized no such place, and the litigants made a compromise. In the last century it has taken its place as the greatest pilgrimage in Ireland. Pilgrims flock there by the thousand, and for three days and two nights endure the austerities, the fasting, and the vigils handed down by the mediaeval tradition.

The pilgrims are required to walk barefoot round the stony beds of the Saints. The island is now beautified by a modern basilica full of the finest Irish glass, which appears to be floating on the waters. One tree, an old sycamore, grows on the island. It is accounted the holiest tree in Ireland, and it is recorded that half a million pilgrims have prayed in its shadow at different times. The lake is full of fine trout, but never a salmon, owing to a curse by Saint Patrick: one day at the stones across the Freg River he had stepped on a sleeping salmon and slipped. Henceforth salmon were never seen in the Lough.

This is the most wonderful corner of Ireland for legend and folklore and for a traditional history into the unplumbed past.

An ideal subject for a painter. Connemara peasants in their primary colors of red, blue, and yellow, typical of Russia rather than of Ireland, with black shawls over their heads and an intensity of religious fervor in their eyes, going through their penance.

I wrote to the Prior telling him that I was an artist and a Belfast Catholic, and should like to come to the island to paint the scene of the pilgrimage. A cordial invitation was given; he was sure God would bless the work, and to his knowledge no painter had ever made a picture of it.

A large four-oared rowing boat capable of holding about twenty pilgrims took us across the short strip of water that lay between the mainland and Saint Patrick's Purgatory. Not being a pilgrim in the strict sense of the word, I was allowed to keep my boots on, a privilege also extended to the Prior, who welcomed me on landing and helped me with my painting outfit to a cold, gray stone building, where he gave me, so far as I could see, the only furnished room in it. I discovered afterwards that it was his own bedroom, and that the three or four nights when I occupied it he had slept in another part of the building on the floor.

My first impression of the pilgrims surprised me. Instead of the picturesque peasants from the west there were the everyday types one would see in the streets of Belfast or Dublin, with only a sprinkling of peasants. Old and young, rich and poor, were deeply engaged in prayer, moving round the seven circles, sometimes on their knees, wet or dry, without intermission, except for the time spent in contemplation and the hearing of Masses. Fasting and prayer for three days and two nights if flesh and blood could stand it. Some who gave in were revived with dry bread and tea without sugar or milk.

The Prior was occupied all the time, except for the brief minutes he gave to our frugal meals, which I was privileged to take with him. I did not like to tell him that my faith did not tempt me to follow the example of the pilgrims, but he could not help seeing that my interest lay in painting a picture, which was, to him, another way of showing the grace of God and another example of His great mercy.

No one seemed to show any interest in what I was doing, and it was only on my way home with one of the pilgrims that I got to understand why educated and uneducated, politician, businessman, shop and factory girls, and even a sprinkling of what are called Society ladies, all found peace. His explanation was simple. He said that if you believed in God and desired to be alone with

Him, there was no other way that he knew of in this world. From the moment he took off his shoes and his bare feet touched the cold earth, until he put them on again, he was in a new world where everything he valued in the world he had left disappeared, and instead came a feeling as if a great load of pain and misery had been lifted. Things of this life became valueless, the horror of death no longer existed, in fact there was no such thing. Each year he returned to the Purgatory and the burden of life became easier to bear and a spirit of buoyancy took its place. I discovered afterwards that he was a professor of science at an English university.

We parted, he going his way and I mine. But I could not help thinking that perhaps there was something to it, and that I might paint better if I took my head out of the paintpot for a moment and thought of other things than trying to paint pictures. The mood did not last. I was no sooner back and had turned out my studies than the problem of picture-making banished everything else. I excused myself on the ground that I had a purgatory of my own, and that to get mixed up with another one would be more than I could bear; and so my good intentions, like so many others I had indulged in, went with the wind or to that place which is said to be paved with them.

While on the subject of miraculous renovation, I should like to mention the one case I know of when a physical miracle occurred. Some years ago my cousin Kate wrote from Ireland to say that her son Eddie was interested in art, and was attending a school in Belfast for the study of sculpture. What would I advise regarding his training? I suggested his coming to London, where I would look after him. A week or so later a young man, slightly lame, looking rather scared and shy, and with a voice so low that I could hardly hear him speak, called to say that he was Eddie Clenaghan and he had got lodgings in Pimlico, from whence he had had great difficulty in finding Cromwell Place. I told him always to ask a policeman should he lose his way again. He said he had done so but that the policeman had failed to hear him, and when he had touched his sleeve to attract attention he had been angry and had said, "Are you aware that if you lay hands on the police you are liable to arrest?" That was before every policeman in London was "wonderful."

I took him round to the Royal College of Art, to my friend Rothenstein, who very kindly interested himself and put him under his professor of sculpture. I told Eddie I thought Paris a better place for a student of sculpture. To my amazement he replied that he had been there on his way to Lourdes. He then explained that once while playing with another boy he had fallen over a cliff and broken his pelvis, and had been in bed for five years, being considered incurable. He had been taken at last to Lourdes on a stretcher, but had come home again in the same manner and been put back to bed. After some weeks he awoke one morning to find that he could move his legs without pain. He rose, and has been able to walk ever since.

I wrote asking Kate if this were all true. She answered, "Every word of it," adding that Eddie's name would have been on the register of miracles had not the bishop responsible for the veracity of the case died before recording the fact. I have often tried to imagine his sensations on that tremendous morning when he found himself cured!

Hazel, who was very keen on the Irish Question, said to me one day, "John, why don't you do something for your country?" Now, an undeveloped sense of patriotism was my trouble. For years I did not seem to grasp what Ireland had suffered, and if I did the feeling was that possibly it served us right. But when the Great War came and the Black and Tans were given carte blanche to do their damnedest, – which they did, – the desire to fight stirred in my blood for the first time. Yet I very much doubt if it was patriotism and a love of country so much as a sense of justice. There was nothing much I could do. So when Hazel asked me why I did not do something for my country I replied, "I cannot see that I can do anything without mixing myself with religion or politics, and I have no time to differ with people." "Don't differ," she replied. "Just agree with them all, as you do anyway." So it struck me that I might be some use in making my studio neutral ground where both sides might meet.

I started painting a triptych with Hazel as the Madonna, Eileen as Saint Brigid, and Alice as the boy Patrick, the swineherd, and presented it as an altarpiece to Saint Patrick's Church in Belfast, where I was baptized. Then, to show the other side that I was not a bigot, I presented them with the original study for the Royal Portrait Group at the National Portrait Gallery. Then I went south and entered the political arena by inviting Edward Carson and John Redmond to sit, on condition that they would allow me to present their portraits to the Dublin Gallery to be hung side by side. They both came and sat, and, as usual, they each thought the other's portrait was the better. Carson, knowing that I was a Catholic, although from Belfast, looking at the two portraits together, remarked, "Ah, it's easy to see which side you're on." Redmond did not criticize, he only said plaintively, "I have always had an idea that Carson and I might some day be hanged side by side in Dublin, and now it has come to pass." When the Free State had been established I painted a second portrait of Carson, for Belfast. He looked at it for a long time and, as if speaking to himself, said, "Well now, you can call that 'Edward Carson after the Surrender.' " I asked Lord D'Abernon for his opinion. "My dear John, you have quite missed the character. It is not like him, you haven't caught the criminal look. No, it's not good." "Well, his wife thinks it's the best portrait that has been done of him." "Yes of course, that damns it."

Hazel thought it a good beginning but she wanted something bigger done. Why not join together all the contending elements of my native city? It was rather a large order, but I started with a light heart. First of all two Archbishops, Cardinal Logue and Archbishop d'Arcy, then the Grand Master of the Orange Lodge, and Joe Devlin, Sir James Craig, Archbishop MacRory, and Bishop Grierson, with a judicious mingling of the others.

Hazel came with me to Armagh to paint the Cardinal, a little old man with round shoulders and his head shot forward, with beetling brows and a long upper lip, indicative, I believe, of humor. Owing to the position of his head it was difficult to see his eyes. Towards the end of the last sitting I said, "Your Eminence, I have not yet seen the color of your eyes." He looked up, and two piercing orbs were brought to bear on me. "They are Irish gray, your Eminence." "No, they are black, or perhaps they have become gray with the years." I doubt if he was pleased with the portrait, for after looking at it for some time he said, "The last artist who painted me made me look like a monkey in a bush." I must admit there was something simian in what I had done. He did not show any resentment, however, and when we were going away paid us both very charming compliments for coming to see a lonely old man. Hazel said, "Your Eminence will forget all about us when we are gone." He replied, "Well, at any rate I'll remember the color of your eyes."

There is a story told of him, in fact they say he tells it himself. When he was a young priest, a girl came to him in confession and after the act of contrition continued, "Father, I have a mortal sin to confess, and I cannot tell it because it is about a priest." "My child, you are not confessing to me alone, you are confessing to God, and if you repent you will be forgiven." "Yes, Father, but when I go to Mass on Sunday and look up at the altar and see you there I can't help thinking, surely that is the ugliest man God ever made."

At Armagh, the headquarters of the two Churches both occupy hills facing each other. When Cromwell arrived there was only one, but he did not like the congregation, so cleared them out and annexed the church, which looks well from the outside, leaving the evicted to seek fresh pastures, which they did by building an edifice exactly opposite the old. There they stand like pillars of Hercules, each with a hill to itself, each claiming to be the seat of the "Primate of All Ireland."

After I had painted the Cardinal, the next in order was the Archbishop. My friends the Londonderrys arranged that I should meet him at Mount Stewart. After the scarlet robes of His Eminence, His Grace in black was not so exciting, but his short gray beard, clipped to a point, reminded me of a type of ecclesiastic I was familiar with in Scotland.

I was halfway through the portrait when I received an anonymous letter, headed in large block capitals "THE LONDONDERRY AIR," and below, the lines from Shelley: —

I met murder on the way —
He had a mask like Castlereagh,
Very smooth he looked, yet grim;
Seven bloodhounds followed him . . .

asking if I had no sense of shame — stating that sycophants and parasites like me should be exterminated like vermin, and more of the same sort. I showed it to Hazel, saying, "That's what comes of doing something for Ireland." She said, "Never mind, carry on."

I could not help thinking what Lord Londonderry must have had to put up with on my account, since it was entirely owing to his support that the Freedom of Belfast and the Honorary Degree at Queen's University came to me. I felt much in his debt, saying that I would remember him in my prayers, a form of repayment which I have always found economical and sometimes impressive.

Before we went to Mount Stewart Hazel had reminded me of Winston's desire to know what I thought of the state of affairs in Ireland. Between us we sent him the following letter: —

My dear Minister of War, —

You asked me the other day what I thought of my country's state, and I had not the courage to tell you.

But if one artist may speak to another I will give you my beliefs.

The Prime Minister has said that he is prepared for a million casualties and a five years' war. I believe that ten million and a fifty years' war would not bring about the result he desires.

I believe that Ireland will never be governed by Westminster, the Vatican, or Ulster without continuous bloodshed.

I also believe that the removal of the "Castle" and all its works, leaving Irishmen to settle their own affairs, is the only solution left.

I am convinced with the knowledge I possess of my countrymen that such a situation would make her one of your staunchest allies instead of an avowed enemy for all time. Love is stronger than hate.

Yours

HAZEL AND JOHN

Things in Dublin were getting pretty bad when an invitation came to Hazel to meet Lloyd George at dinner at Sir Philip Sassoon's.

"Now is your chance," said I to Hazel, "to do something for Ireland."

When she returned she said that he was a wizard right enough. He had made her feel so interested in herself that the Irish Question was put in the background. She had never met anyone with greater charm, and she was sure of his sympathetic treatment of the Irish. Next morning she read in *The Times* that "Lloyd George had the trouble well in hand," and that some thousand Black and Tans had landed and were driving all before them. "Terrifying the rebels into submission and getting their own back."

She was so disappointed that some time afterwards, when an official letter came stating that the Prime Minister desired to place my name before the King as one deserving recognition, she counseled declining the honor on the ground that "Mr." was more distinguished than "Sir." But "Lady Lavery" had a pleasing sound, so I accepted — men always blame their wives on such occasions. We both wondered who had been working to bring the distinction about, and it is only now that it occurs to me the idea must have been inaugurated that night at Philip Sassoon's.

England and Ireland were at war, Black and Tans and Republicans. I told Winston that I was going to Ireland to paint Michael Collins. "Be careful, my dear John, our men are not all good shots." But I was not able to go, and even if I had been I didn't quite see how my sitter could have been expected to sit. At last the Treaty Negotiations were under way. Hazel got in touch with Collins's sister, and one morning he walked into my studio, a tall young Hercules with a pasty face, sparkling eyes, and a fascinating smile. I helped him off with a heavy overcoat to which he clung, excusing himself by saying casually, "There is a gun in the pocket."

He came over, as everyone knows, on a safe-conduct with Griffith, Gavan Duffy, Barton, Duggan, and Erskine Childers. De Valera had been over a week or two before but had failed to come to terms, and now sent these representatives in the hope that a treaty might result. De Valera came to sit for a couple of hours. I was naturally more interested in what he looked like than in what he said — something to the effect that the mass of the people are like sheep in that they run after each other. I cannot remember what called forth the remark — the statement was not new to me. My regret is that I had so little time to paint him.

I had more time with his delegates. Hazel was anxious that they should meet Englishmen of importance concerned with the Irish Question, and this resulted in many dinner parties and other functions. But there was one delegate who held out — Erskine Childers. I had him on the telephone once or twice, but he would not be induced to come, not even to a meal.

By many it was believed that had it not been for Hazel there would have been no Treaty — certainly not at the time it was signed. She had given up Erskine Childers as impossible to move, but she had overcome Arthur Griffith's objections. Michael Collins stood firm to the last minute. He seemed to have lost his temper. Even I, whose head was never really out of the paintpot, could see that he who loses his temper in argument is lost, and told him so, but I failed to convince him. Eventually, after hours of persuasion, Hazel prevailed. She took him to Downing Street in her car that last evening, and he gave in. Yet he knew, knowing our queer race, that in signing he might well be signing his death warrant. Neither friend nor foe ever accused this man of lacking courage.

One night at dinner Hazel had on one side of her Lord French and on the other Michael Collins. Looking across at him, Lord French said, "This is the first time I have had the pleasure of meeting you, Mr. Collins." "It is not the first time I have seen your Lordship," said Collins, "for a couple of months ago you were by yourself near the Lodge and the boys surrounded you, but I called them off, I thought it so brave of you." "London," said French, "is the best place, after all, to meet people. For a considerable time I was on the heels of De Wet in South Africa and only caught up with him in London here, at dinner."

Winston invited me with Collins to luncheon. He showed us some interesting things, among which was a copy of a South African poster which read: "£10 Reward for Winston Churchill, dead or alive." "We put a bigger price on you, Mr. Collins," said Winston; "I think it was £10,000." "Prices have gone up since your day, Mr. Churchill."

Collins was a patient sitter, but I noticed that he liked to sit facing the door. He was always on the alert. During the war in Ireland he was almost a wizard in the way he was never caught. He did not go into hiding, yet when the military came to some house they had seen him enter they never could find him, though there seemed no means of escape — in this and the capacity to disguise himself he bore a strong resemblance to Lenin, I am told. He told me that his mother died during the troubles, and that he insisted on going to her funeral. His friends implored him not to, for it would be putting himself into the hands of the military. But he went. And the military went. He stood in their midst. But they could not see him — so skillful was his make-up as a monk.

It was interesting to note how he and Lord Birkenhead took to one another. Collins had a great admiration for the extraordinary facility of Birkenhead's address, and the un-English directness of his phraseology on occasion. No one could be as successfully insulting to "Noble Lords" as the "Galloper." Collins would have delighted in the occasion when, during the debate on the Treaty, the pale face of Lord Carson grew steadily paler as he listened to the heightening invective of Birkenhead, which reached at last to the words, "The solution of this problem advanced by the Noble Lord would sound immature on the lips of an hysterical schoolgirl!" Many a morning before the Downing Street meetings Collins would be seen hurrying to meet Birkenhead. No one knows what took place.

When the delegates returned to Dublin, Hazel and I also went over. We now learnt that Collins had "sold his country." Phrases are terrible things — why not hang every person who coins a dangerous one and impose a fine of £10 for a silly one? One day we lunched with Collins at the Gresham Hotel. On his way there he was ordered to put his hands up by a youth with a gun. In putting them up he knocked the youth over and took the gun from him, telling him that he had stopped the wrong man, together with a few other points the youth had overlooked. They shook hands and parted friends, Michael keeping the gun.

One evening he came to dine with us at the Kingstown Hotel. I did not know till afterwards that Hazel had saved his life by sitting for half an hour between him and the window where a gunman had been placed. She was anxious that he should meet Horace Plunkett and took him there the same evening alone. I was a little anxious, but for some reason did not go. Coming back they were waylaid and half a dozen shots were poured into the car. I examined it with an electric torch and it seemed a miracle that no one was hurt, for there were six people in the car, sitting close together. The bullets must have gone over their heads. Collins made light of it, but complained of a pain in his side that he thought might possibly be his appendix. After much persuasion he accepted my hot-water bottle, and placing it under his tunic he smilingly said that the pain had gone. With a "God bless you both," he jumped into his car with Emmet Dalton and Joe Riley, dashing off into the night. That was the last I saw of him alive.

Hazel was pale with excitement and woke up screaming once or twice that night. Next day she was strange and silent. I could not get her to talk. She had fearful premonitions. Once, after a dinner party, she had told me that Sargent, who was present, was about to die — and he died. Now she said at last, looking away from me, "All day I have been seeing them carrying Michael covered with blood. Wherever I go I cannot get rid of the sight." I got her to bed and sat with her until well on into the night, and at last she went to sleep. At seven in the morning her very English maid came in with the tea. After she had put it down she said in a voice showing not the slightest trace of interest, "They have shot Mr. Collins, my lady."

I felt then, and feel still, that on that night the Irish slew the Irish they killed Ireland as a force for good and greatness in the world of to-day, when every horror is committed in the name of nationalism.

His body was brought back to Dublin and placed in the mortuary chapel, where only relatives and closest friends were admitted. I was allowed to paint him in death. Any grossness in his features, even the peculiar little dent near the point of his nose, had disappeared. He might have been Napoleon in marble as he lay in his uniform, covered by the Free State flag, with a crucifix on his breast. Four soldiers stood round the bier. The stillness was broken at long intervals by someone entering the chapel on tiptoe, kissing the brow, and then slipping to the door, where I could hear a burst of suppressed grief. One woman kissed the dead lips, making it hard for me to continue my work.

All day I strove to record the mystery that seemed to play about that mouth, the lips appearing to move at times. When I got back to Kingstown at midnight the hotel was all dark; the night porter let me in — the one who had told me of the gunman at the window two nights previously. I thought it would interest him to see what I had done, so, opening up the picture, I placed it on a chair under a light in the hall. He looked long, and in a harsh, strange voice said, "Well now, that is the last of Mike; the next one will get the same." "Are you an Irishman?" I asked. "I am, God help me." "I hope he will," I said. I have often been told of the treachery of my countrymen by those who did not like them, but this was the first experience of it at the source. I now believe that I misunderstood what he said, and that he really meant there were so many misguided people that no one trying to save his country would be allowed to live. How then can Ireland live? Must she not herself be slain if she slew, in Gogarty's great phrase, "the most rapid and bright soul that alien envy ever quenched"?

Over against that I should, however, like to place Bernard Shaw's letter to Collins's sister. It strikes a more hopeful note. Of one thing I am certain — Shaw has never written a letter to a bereaved person without giving courage, master of natural psychology that he is.

MY DEAR MISS COLLINS, —

Don't let them make you miserable about it: how could a born soldier die better than at the victorious end of a good fight, falling to the shot of another Irishman — a damned fool, but all the same an Irishman who thought he was fighting for Ireland — "a Roman to a Roman"?

I met Michael for the first and last time on Saturday last, and am very glad I did. I rejoice in his memory, and will not be so disloyal to it as to snivel over his valiant death.

So tear up your mourning and hang up your brightest colors in his honor; and let us all praise God that he had not to die in a snuffy bed of a trumpery cough, weakened by age, and saddened by the disappointments that would have attended his work had he lived.

Sincerely
BERNARD SHAW

August 24th, 1922

One Sunday morning, some months after Michael Collins's death, Kevin O'Higgins, perhaps the greatest diplomat of them all and the one pillar of strength left, was shot down on his way to Mass. The following letter to Hazel makes even sadder reading now than it did when she received it.

BAILE ATHA CLIATH
1/9/22

DEAR LADY LAVERY, –

Your letter of Wednesday reached me here yesterday. I have been recalled from the Army and have been asked to take on "Home Affairs." I can well imagine how greatly shocked you must have been at the tragic news. There are times when the only safety-valve is work, things so terrible that one dare not stop to think on them. There is work enough to our hands, God knows, and there is the clear duty to carry on and endeavor to save Michael's achievements for the country from destruction.

. . . Childers is no fool. He knows that when he destroys property, bridges, railways, etc., he infuriates the people, but he is prepared to go on infuriating them, hoping for a social and economic collapse, hoping for a point when the people will kick out blindly at an intolerable condition – *qua* intolerable condition – regardless of the question of who caused it. He and De Valera know that their following is mainly criminal, in motive and in act, but they are prepared to go on using that criminal instrument in the hope of crumbling foundations. This is ghoulish – but I think it is true.

On the whole I think the odds are against their success – the next two months will decide that. Our Parliament meets on the 9th. Is there any chance of seeing yourself and Sir John on that occasion? I wish I could write you in cheerier vein, but the position is too grim. Of course it was grim before – the winter of 1920, for instance – and we weathered it. One thing you may be sure of – there will be no quitting, and no trifling with the bond of the two who are gone. We will get on with the work – and *you*, whom Michael loved so well, will pray for our success, and will help when you can in the way that only *you* can. I wish you could realize how much all here appreciate your help and sympathy.

Greetings,

KEVIN O'HIGGINS

It was one of O'Higgins's ambitions that Hazel should be in the Vice-Regal Lodge. He carried the measure in London, the week before he died, but I very much doubt if it would have passed the Dail. A couple of days before he was shot – and they went on pouring lead into him as he lay on the ground – I met Winston, who said, "Well, John, are you getting ready?" Pretending that I did not know what he meant, I said, "Ready for what?" "The Vice-Regal." "That's a dream of O'Higgins's," I said. "Anyway, we are in favor of it here," answered Winston.

I must say I was very much surprised and, of course, swollen up with pride that it had really gone so far. On the other hand, Ireland is a great country for prejudice and fault-finding against institutions such as Viceroys and Governor Generals. I think we have too much sense of humor to go in for that sort of thing with the seriousness of the English. I remember when Tim Healy was appointed, someone mentioned it to A.E. "Useless expense," was the poet's curt and Irish reply.

Hazel's first sight of the "Lodge" was when she went to stay with the Wimbornes. She was thrilled by its beauty, which reminded her of the White House and the eighteenth century she loved. From that moment there was no other Ireland for her. She wandered about Ireland in a dream, finding out that she was really Irish; the Martyns of Galway were her people, and it was purely by accident of birth that America claimed her. When she first met Edward Martyn she told him this. He looked at her and said, "You can't be a relation of mine, we never had a beautiful woman in our family yet." He hated women. She could not rest until she had explored every corner of the land. To her it was the Ireland of Yeats, James Stephens, A.E., Lennox Robinson, Synge, and the rest. Hazel's Ireland was as unreal as a mirage in the desert.

Although we received many anonymous and threatening letters, I do not believe that there was a youth in Ireland so misguided as to turn his gun on a woman. Had she been allowed to reign and had her health held out, she might have succeeded. I should have been no use.

I had vague thoughts of Velásquez as Ambassador for Philip IV, Vandyke and other artists in diplomatic positions, but saw the absurdity of it all so far as it concerned me, and told Kevin so. There could have been no one more unfitted for the post than I, believing as I do that the more nations and religions there are, the greater the opportunities for disorder.

Hazel broke down when Kevin was assassinated. Apart from the tragedy, it shattered her dream of the Vice-Regal Lodge. I was terribly sorry for her, for if there ever was a woman qualified for the position of Vicereine of Ireland at that period it was Hazel. When I realized her disappointment I felt I could have given up the paint-brush for the simple joy of seeing her great gifts gloriously framed for the benefit of the Ireland of her own creation, which may indeed have been the real Ireland. At the same time I had a selfish sense of relief that the life I had lived for over half a century, and the one for which I was best fitted, was not to be disturbed.

After O'Higgins's death Mr. Cosgrave and the currency commission hit on the idea of recognizing Hazel's services, and commissioned me to paint her portrait to be reproduced on the bank notes which, as President Cosgrave in his charming way said, "every Irishman, not to mention the foreigner who visits Ireland, will carry next to his heart."

She admired Cosgrave and realized that no other statesman could have done what he did in bringing Ireland in touch with the rest of the world, and forming out of the chaos the most stable government in Europe at the time. To rise up as he had done, in the midst of a bloody revolution, without any of the machinery of a governing body, to bring together in peaceful conference men whose chief argument was the gun, was an achievement of which history can show few to equal. But for him Hazel's memory in Ireland might be soon forgotten.

There was one Englishman whose name seldom appeared in print, but who was working night and day behind the scenes to bring about a settlement. He was the liaison officer between the two countries, known to his friends as "Andy" Cope and to the world as Sir Alfred Cope, K.C.B., and so forth, Assistant Under-Secretary for Ireland, and Clerk of the Privy Council. In the following letter to Hazel he includes me, but he was mistaken, as were many others, in giving me credit for work I cannot lay claim to, and for virtues that I do not possess.

18 Abingdon Street
Westminster, S.W. 1
30-6-23

Dear Lady Lavery, —

I want to thank you and Sir John very sincerely for your kindness to me last night, and indeed the many kindnesses you have shown me throughout the time I have had the good fortune to know you. Forgive my saying so, but I have closely watched the work you and Sir John have set out to accomplish, from the first day we met (when Winston hurried me round to your house). You are two wonderful people carrying out in a wonderful way a truly gigantic task

– the task of getting Protestant England to see some virtue in Catholic Ireland. This is indeed a most gigantic task, full of disappointments and perils for those who undertake it, and I speak from experience. It is a great task but it has a great goal, and though you and Sir John may never see its accomplishment, yet you have taken it a long way towards the desired end and you have my sincerest good wishes. The difficulty of the task lies in the fact that Protestant England has deep-rooted antipathies towards Catholic Ireland. I expected it from the first but always hoped against it, but now with much reluctance I am forced to accept it. However, I am convinced that these antipathies *can* be removed, and that you and Sir John are traveling the *only* road to remove them. England is slow-moving, and just as she is slow to transfer her affections so she is slow to remove her hatreds. I wish it were otherwise in the case of Catholic Ireland. Shortly after I arrived in Ireland I set myself the same task that you have undertaken, and in accepting my present job I thought I might get a better opportunity of pursuing my ideal. But I am afraid I have been brought to a temporary halt – temporary, I truly hope and believe – for my attachment to a really great but sadly maligned statesman has clipped my wings and I must wait for them to grow again. But you and Sir John can and must go on, for you are doing *big* things and your power to do big things is increasing daily.

As for last night. It was magnificent. It was an experience for me that will fill my thoughts for weeks to come. There were small men and small women, and great men and great women. And among the men stood out *Winston;* how big he seems to me and how pleased I was that although the Irish

Treaty was mainly responsible for his fall from office, yet he gave me a cheery welcome. And also among what I feel to be the great ones, there were Sir John and yourself working with splendid anxiety towards the great end.

More when I see you.

Ever yours sincerely,

A. Cope

XVIII

AMERICA

Eddie Knoblock told me that America is to many the "Land of Promise," to many more the "Land of Promises"; to me it is a rich man surrounded by sycophants and adventurers from all parts of the globe ready to fill their pockets. To go unaccredited to America is to place oneself in the above category and to be treated accordingly, but to go accredited is to find the most hospitable, generous, and simple-minded people that I have lived amongst.

An artist friend who had just returned from New York, where he had painted half a dozen portraits, recommended to me a nice, quiet, comfortable hotel not at all expensive. The last qualification appealed to me, as we were a party of five – Hazel, Alice, a maid, a valet who was also chauffeur-secretary, and myself, so I was pleased to find that I could have a suite on the first floor for thirty dollars a day. On our arrival an old American friend of mine was waiting for us. He was very cordial, and taking me aside said, "My dear fellow, you can't stay here, you can't afford to." I was a little nettled. "Oh, I don't think it's so expensive." "No, that's not what I mean; the Prince of Wales couldn't risk it. No, you must go to the Ritz or the Ambassador. You must appear as though money were no object." The Ambassador had a sound of opulence about it, so we went there. There was a highly titled English family of moderate means in the suite above us, and we gathered from the eggshells dropped each morning on our back balcony on their way to the yard below that the hotel restaurant was not being patronized by them, but rather the delicatessen shop round the corner.

It was during Prohibition, and the hospitable Americans were sorely put to it to entertain their guests. Even millionaires were at the mercy of the bootlegger. Among all my sitters there was only one who was a real Prohibitionist, and he made believe that he was not by a homemade brew he offered his guests as Burgundy. I shall never forget Osbert Sitwell's face when he went to dine there. I had been telling him that at no time had I seen drink flow so generously as at American tables, and that our host would be no exception. I doubt if he can ever forgive me that homemade Burgundy. Osbert likes Burgundy – I don't.

There were terrifying tales of the poisonous stuff to be got in speakeasies, and "blind drunk" had a horrible significance. Cocaine was given in cocktails. I had only one experience of it, and I must admit it was delightful. My conversation had never seemed so brilliant. It was at a large dinner party, and my one regret was that I had to confine my profound remarks to my own end of the table and that everyone could not get the benefit of them. On the way home Hazel told me I had been the laughing-stock of the party. Next morning my head explained the cause – I had been doped. Never again. In so far as "excess leads to the palace of wisdom," Prohibition certainly advanced the cause of sobriety. Whilst it was on, everyone got drunk to excess and had a lesson; now it is off, milk bars and soft drinks have returned. It was also a psychological necessity, I am told, giving the robust citizens of that energetic nation something to disobey and let off their steam against. It could never have been meant seriously on its face value. Inhibition is bad, but Prohibition was mad.

I admire the American attitude towards the Jews. Everywhere I have been, except perhaps in England, the Jew is outcast, and all because of business. My experience is that he is on the whole a more honest man to deal with than some Christians I have met. In Morocco the Jew wears a distinguishing dress and there is no name bad enough for him; even the beaters when pigsticking call to the pig in cover, "Out, Jew!" Every kind of indignity is heaped upon him, and yet there are few people who show a keener appreciation of art or have done more to help the artist. On my return from Germany, thirty years ago, I sat beside a Berlin lady at dinner. She asked who my sitters were, and I gave her a list of names. "Why, they are all Jews! Do you like them?" I answered in jest, "Well, you see, I am a Jew." She was so blinded by prejudice that she believed me and turned her back.

In America the Jew is held in more respect, although classed with negroes and banned in some hotels and clubs because he has joined up with the Irish, and, I believe, has enough political power to overthrow a government. Cardinal Hayes told me that when he returned from Rome, bearing the Hat, one of the most enthusiastic receptions he received was from the Chief Rabbi of New York. It was a new sensation for me to hear a Cardinal speak with a strong American accent; Irish or Italian had been my experience up till then. In speaking of Irish emigrants he said, "We are more sympathetic to them than to any other nationality." Recently a poor Irish girl had been sent to Ellis Island as an undesirable alien. She asked why, and was told she was anaemic and unfit for work. She replied, "Well now, if you had nothing on your stomach for three weeks but your two cold hands *you* would be anaemic." She was admitted.

When I was painting the Cardinal, Malvina Hoffman very kindly lent me her studio. I heard that Mrs. Havemeyer had a Spanish cardinal by El Greco, so, as I was anxious to get some hints from the Spanish master, I got permission to see the picture. Mrs. Havemeyer was ill and deputed her housekeeper to show me round. When she found I was an Irish Catholic and painting Cardinal Hayes she nearly wept on my shoulder. I told her the El Greco I sought was an early portrait of a Cardinal with a beard. "And what would a Catholic Cardinal be doing in this house? Surely it is a Protestant Cardinal," said the housekeeper. "Oh no, the Protestant Church goes the length of an Archbishop and stops there. This is not only a Catholic Cardinal, but he belongs to a country whose King is His Most Catholic Majesty." She crossed herself. "God forgive me, I thought it was John Knox."

I was struck on my last visit by the cordiality and friendliness of the people in every station of life, especially out West. In some of the restaurants and hotels there is a notice, "Gratuities are forbidden." This gave me great pleasure and a feeling of equality shared by the servants. It is hard to think of anything more degrading than "tipping" for all concerned. It is unfair to those of limited means that this system of bribery should be tolerated.

Here at home I am often asked such questions as, "What do you think of America?" "Did it make your blood boil to see how they have robbed us of our art treasures?" I saw the art treasures all right, and beautifully cared for, but I did not think of the robbery as such, knowing the large sums that were paid for them. There are various ways of acquiring art treasures, and the thought of the Elgin Marbles comes to me.

During the four or five winters I spent in the States I am ashamed to say that except in Pittsburgh I never had the opportunity of visiting any of the annual exhibitions of contemporary art and am therefore not in the position to express an opinion, although I saw an outdoor exhibition of modern sculpture last year, some of considerable merit, which made me still more regret that lack of time forbade my seeing the modern galleries. Of the artists I was familiar with thirty years ago many are gone and the work of others has not survived the test of time.

In Paris, in the eighties, Whistler, Sargent, E. A. Abbey, John W. Alexander, Sprague Pierce, Dannat, Chase, Augustus Saint-Gaudens, Harrison, Winslow Homer, were names I was familiar with. Few of them remain to-day. There was one woman painter whose work was in advance of her time and was on a par with the best French Impressionists, and that was Mary Cassatt, who came on the scene as I was leaving Paris. I remember, too, Cecilia Beaux as a follower of Sargent, and later Malvina Hoffman, a pupil of Rodin, one of the finest women sculptors of her age. Another friend, but in this case one who owes nothing to Paris, is Clara Fargo Thomas, who has done some interesting murals and whose study "Pax Britannica" is one of the most brilliant designs for a mural on shipping that I can remember.

My first visit to America was in 1898, when I sat on the jury of awards at the Carnegie Art Institute in Pittsburgh. Three thousand dollars were awarded in prizes between Dwight W. Tryon, Childe Hassam, and Alexander Roche, while E. A. Walton and John F. Weir received Honorable Mention. A new world of artists is working with us to-day, with whose work I am unfamiliar.

For over thirty years Pittsburgh, owing to the munificence of the late Mr. Carnegie, has gathered together the best annual collection of contemporary art that an international jury with unlimited means at its disposal could select. This was — and is — sent on loan all over the States, even to New York itself. The result has been that every city of importance has its public gallery where the works of European artists may be seen. By inviting artists of European fame to send to America free of all cost examples of their best work; by making rewards of a monetary value never before attempted in any country; by the purchase of works on a scale that is both just and generous, Pittsburgh has rendered an inestimable service to both painters and public. The man at the head of all this is Homer Saint-Gaudens, to whom America is indebted for that rare combination, an instinct for what is finest in art and an organizing ability unsurpassed.

Of the number of private collections, headed by those of Mr. Clarence Mackay and Mr. Frick of New York, Mr. Widener of Philadelphia, and others, words fail me to give a hint of their riches in every department of art work. I came away from the Widener collection with the feeling that I had never seen pictures and *objets d'art* under better conditions. Now to-day we read of the gift to Washington of the Mellon collection, the like of which history fails to record.

Behind many of these collectors stood the late Sir Joseph Duveen of Millbank. It is to him that America owes much in her present-day collections of masterpieces, and to him that England is indebted for the reconstruction of the Tate Gallery, the National Portrait Gallery, and for the new galleries in the British Museum, including his many gifts of ancient and modern masterpieces to London and the provinces.

I have not been to Washington, the most beautiful city in America, St. Louis, Brooklyn, or to many other galleries scattered throughout the States, but from what I hear I can accept them as justifying America's claim to a place in the sun.

I was much impressed by Chicago, on my first visit to Hazel's birthplace. We were met at the station by the whole colony of professional painters, numbering six or seven, who entertained us with true American hospitality. That was twenty-five years ago — to-day it is very different. We were taken to the Art School where there were over a hundred girls and young men, doing work that would shame the same number of students in any other school I know. I could never understand why it was that Chicago could only provide work for a very few professional artists and what happened to all those gifted young people. The explanation given to me at the time was that the students for the most part married, some drifted into black-and-white work, the illustrated journals being superior to those of Europe, others towards murals, but a very great number gave it up. This latter reason I could not understand, in the face of such accomplishment as the majority of them possessed.

It was great joy to me last year to find modern pictures in great numbers at the Chicago Art Institute beautifully shown under the best conditions of lighting and color. The Metropolitan Museum in New York looked dull in comparison. Whistler's "Henry Irving as Philip II" might have been painted when the sweeps were at work, as the critics said of his "Little White Girl," greatly owing to the position given it on a dark wall.

Education runs rampant in America. Without exception everyone I met, from statesmen to workmen, had had a college or university education. Dr. Nicholas Murray Butler, President of Columbia University, a scholar of international fame, has done much, aided by the Carnegie and Rockefeller endowments, to make such a thing possible.

Lecturers from Europe who speak English abound, dealing with every possible subject under the sun. One qualification they must have is to be able to speak without notes: the moment he or she looks at a paper the audience get restive and go. Agents arrange these tours on commission, a pretty high one according to the business capacities of the lecturer. A Royal prince and the brother of a king, who had been in the Foreign Legion, told me with pride that he was paid $100 a lecture, while a shrewd literary friend of mine was receiving $1000. Years ago titles fetched big prices, to-day they are so much a dozen. It is much the same on the Riviera. There, people were raising their hats to a tall gentleman who was passing. I asked who he might be. The answer I got was, "*Un souverain quelconque*." As for the knights, they did not count at all. I was invariably addressed as "Sir Lavery." In the *New York Times*, when Austen Chamberlain received the Order of the Garter, it was announced, "Austen Chamberlain dubbed knight by George." I was interviewed by a newshawk, a fellow countryman of mine, on the subject, and explained to him that it was not a mere knighthood, but the highest honor the King could bestow. All I found next day was, "Lavery, dubbed knight by three Kings." *Erin go bragh!*

The Royal prince I mentioned was Prince Aage of Denmark. He had been for some months working as a stoker on a tramp steamer before joining the Foreign Legion. When he came to see us in Tangier we tried hard to keep him out of the clutches of the crooks that abounded there, mostly bogus landowners. He was not there a week before he brought up thousands of acres that did not exist, at half their supposed value, emptying his pockets and leaving himself committed up to the hilt. He said his aunt would pay for him. He would tell her, he added with a laugh, that he had been dealing in real estate that was not real.

Portrait painting in America differs from that art everywhere else. If you are accredited you can do and say what you like and it will be accepted. I was often asked, when completing a picture, if it was the best I had done. If it was seen that I was at all diffident in the matter, disappointment was apparent. I tried sometimes to avoid a direct answer by quoting Josh Billings, when he wrote: "I knew he was a gentleman because he told me so himself, and he wouldn't lie about a little thing like that." I gave up quoting Josh because it seemed to displease, and I got to think that Americans in some things were different to us. I could not imagine being asked such a thing at home until one day I found myself putting the same kind of question to my tailor. Had he replied, "Well now, that reminds me," and so on, I doubt if I should have thought it very funny. But I must say Americans do seem to lack a sense of humor in personal and national matters. Once, in an after-dinner speech in New York, I told my audience of an incident that had happened to me on arrival, thinking that it might be appropriate and appreciated. I had got on a streetcar (as omnibuses are called) and asked the conductor to put me down at Fifth Avenue. "Yap!" he said. I thought he said "What?" so I asked him again, speaking very slowly and distinctly. He was taking dimes and punching tickets, and without looking up he said, "Keep your shirt on, I'll lay you down gently." Having delivered this carefully prepared anecdote at the dinner party, I waited for a good loud round of applause and laughter. It didn't go down at all well. When I stepped from the platform two or three people came up to me and one said, "Now, sir, when you next tell that story you might say the conductor was an Irishman." The Americans have little sense of humor when it is directed at themselves, less even than the Irish. The Scot is the only man in the world who encourages jokes at his own expense.

Once I lost all sense of shame and unblushingly admitted to a persistent sitter that his was the best portrait I had ever painted. His pleasure was almost more than I could bear. Shortly afterwards I had an indignant letter from another client telling me that he had been told to "scrap" the picture I had painted of him, as it was not my best, Mr. N. had got that!

Perhaps the most intelligent portrait commission I ever had came from a Southern state when I was in New York. A man wanted his wife painted but he was not familiar with my work, having only seen a reproduction of a portrait in a magazine. He liked my style, what was my fee, would I come South and paint her? Unfortunately I could not spare the time to visit him, but if his wife would come to New York I would paint her. He accepted my terms but wrote that she would come on condition that if he did not like the portrait I would accept one quarter of my fee and keep the work. If he liked it he would pay a quarter more. She would give me two sittings a day for a week. They came, and it turned out that they were newly married. She was young and beautiful, and in three days I did a most successful portrait. They were both delighted, but I still had three more days to spare and I thought I had better go one better and make a masterpiece of it. The next day it did not go so well, and on the following day I saw that I was spoiling it, but they still liked it. On the last day I was desperate, and utterly ruined it as a work of art. I did not know what to do when he handed me a check for a half more than had been agreed upon. I ran into the next room and told Hazel, who at once said, "Don't show you are not satisfied with it, they would be terribly disappointed. Accept the check and say you would like to paint another portrait and give them their choice." She was so beautiful that this was quite true. It pleased them very much and they arranged to come to New York the following winter, when I painted a picture I was not ashamed of. They did not like it and with some reluctance agreed to accept it as a gift, telling me that the longer they lived with the first the more wonderful they found it.

In those days money was valuable when it could purchase something unique. I was once offered a large sum by a patron if I would decline all further commissions for a certain type of picture of which he wanted a monopoly. Strange to say the remote possibility of being a dollar millionaire had no attraction, although most of my life had been a fight against poverty. In America money seemed to have lost its value. Everyone knows that if you touch a man on his pocket you touch him on a vital spot, whether he be Jew or Gentile. We swear at the American and his almighty dollar, yet I have heard less talk about money there than I do here. It is true that you may hear talk among the poor, as I found at the Waldorf-Astoria, where I went to see a room decorated by Simmons, a student friend of mine. On my way up, the elevator attendant asked if I would like to see a very interesting room "where Jay Gould gave his forty-thousand-dollar dinner." Although for some years I have solved the bread-and-butter problem, when I hear of men I have known in affluence to be the next day in poverty I cannot help feeling a little nervous. Only those who have tasted poverty and bad health can know what it means to have both and at the same time.

It was during our first visit to Chicago, in 1912, that Hazel and I were taken round a motion-picture studio by a large blonde with a bandaged arm and scarred face. She had been put out of action in the shooting of a film called *Lost in the Jungle*. She was supposed to be attacked by a panther and saved by an elephant which, on a former occasion, she had befriended. The panther had been trained to leap for a piece of meat outside the picture, but appeared to be pouncing on the heroine, who had stumbled beside it. At the same moment the friendly elephant rushed in, beat the panther off with its trunk, and placed the prostrate girl on its back. It had all been well rehearsed, but unfortunately, when the final shooting took place, the panther sprang on the girl. Of course there were the usual red-hot bars ready for an emergency, but she was badly scarred.

We were taken to the cutting room and saw the incident thrown on the screen.

Those were the days when the silent pictures were called the "flickers," and flickers they were. I got anxious about my eyes, and on a visit to Wiesbaden, where I had gone to paint Herr von Meister, the *Regierenz Präsident*, with his *gnädige Frau*, I took the opportunity to consult the great oculist, Pagenstaker. He looked into my eyes very carefully, then asked what was the matter. I said I had come to find that out and that I was an artist. He simply said, "Go to an optician. You are an artist – avoid moving pictures. *Auf Wiedersehen.* My fee is ten marks." An English specialist would have charged as many guineas.

It was in the hotel at Wiesbaden that Hazel, whose German was no better than mine, said to the chambermaid, "*Bitte bringen Sie mir viel heisses Wasser, ich will mein Herr waschen.*" She wanted to wash her hair.

XIX

HOLLYWOOD

KING GEORGE V once graciously permitted Buckingham Palace to be used as a film studio in the interests of charity, at a time, moreover, when he was lying seriously ill. I went one day to see the "shooting of a set." It was a scene in the Council Chamber where a dozen society ladies were supposed to be discussing the best means of getting up funds. I was greatly impressed by the extraordinary brilliance of the coloring when the full strength of the powerful lights was on. They made the dullest subjects rainbow-hued. It was then that I thought of Hollywood and its possibilities for the painter. I was told that I should get numerous opportunities for painting any scene I might hit on, because the shooting of the same scene sometimes went on for weeks. When I got to Hollywood, in 1936, I found this to be not quite according to facts as the lighting effects were changing all the time; what at one minute was black darkness was the next brilliantly lighted. Until then I could not understand why it was that all the stars I spoke to complained of the unending repetition of the script long after they knew their parts, and wished themselves out of it in spite of the gold they were amassing, in spite too of the "fans" at their feet, treating them with greater awe and reverence than is given to the rulers of the earth.

My first introductions were to Maureen O'Sullivan and Loretta Young, both of surpassing beauty allied with intelligence and grace of manner. Poets dwell on Irish eyes — Maureen's justify all that has been written about them.

I had hitherto avoided the abnormal child. Coming home some years ago, I overheard two little things of five and six addressing the deck steward. "Say, steward, where's the movie?" "There ain't a movie on this ship." "Say, what's the big idea?" they inquired with one voice. Shirley Temple is very different from that type of American child; in her there is no sign of anything other than innocent childhood allied with the most perfect manners — others addressed me as "Sir Lavery," she, invariably, as "Sir John." I could see from her parents where her intelligence came from.

When I first arrived at the Plaza Hotel, Hollywood, I found an invitation from Alison Skipworth to luncheon at the Paramount Studios. The last time I had seen her was in Glasgow, in 1888, as Alice Groom demonstrating art work at Doulton's stall in the Exhibition. She had been a fascinating, red-haired beauty, attracting crowds by her dexterity in decorating vases. At Paramount she seemed to be a great favorite with the other stars, who called her "Skippy." She introduced me to many of them, including Marlene Dietrich, Herbert Marshall, Rod La Rocque, and others. I made my first attempt at putting something on canvas there. Marlene Dietrich was filming in a Russian play. She was very charming; she told me that she had sat for painters in Germany and she would give me every spare minute of her time. We decided to begin at once, beside the set, so as to be at hand when called. Everyone was most obliging – clearing a space for me to work and setting up a standard lamp to shine on my canvas so that I should be independent of the changing lights from the set. During the War I had got accustomed to all sorts of difficulties in making pictures, but after the first morning at the Paramount Studios I saw there were new problems to solve that I had not been prepared for. The awful confusion, directors, producers, scenario writers, the dozens of camera men, sound recorders, scene shifters, not to speak of actors and actresses, "stand-ins," and extras. Lights on, lights off – "Cut! Cut!" repeated in a loud voice until one wondered if there would be anything left – the wails of the author – bells ringing and a babel of noises – suddenly the director's voice raised above it all – "Silence, please!" Then you might hear a pin drop, afraid to breathe or move while voices were being recorded. I would stand paralyzed until relief came. Then Marlene would rush in and take up her pose in front of her make-up glass. After a couple of mornings I gave it up, determined to make more suitable arrangements when I got to know more of the conditions.

Lady Ravensdale had given me a letter of introduction to Irving Thalberg and half a dozen of the great ones, including Marion Davies, Charlie Chaplin, and the

"World's Sweetheart." I found they were all so surrounded by barbed-wire entanglements in the shape of secretaries that, in spite of a coronet emblazoned on the envelope in which I enclosed my notes, none except that to Mr. Thalberg got further than the secretary's wastepaper basket. In the case of "Charlie" I was told not to post the letter as he never saw letters, but to find out where he was and go myself and present it. I did so, but I was met with, "He is engaged, but if you will leave the letter I will let you know by telephone when he may be seen." That was the last of it.

But I did make an appointment with Irving Thalberg, at M-G-M Studios. When I got there I found an immense shed, one of a dozen covering perhaps a hundred acres. In it there were part of a ballroom, a street, a lake, real cypress trees with their tops cut, half a stairway, a balcony, and in the distance, in semidarkness, a sound record being made of disconnected scraps of conversation. In one corner there was a whole crowd of men and women, children, dwarfs, and courtiers all in the most gorgeous Florentine costumes, some mounted on magnificently caparisoned horses. They were all standing as stock-still as the horses and hounds would permit, in absolute silence, in the dazzling, blazing light, waiting for their cue to dash through a half-formed arch leading nowhere. The whole set was seen through a network of iron cranes with camera men, light projectors, and sound recorders perched upon them.

This was my first impression of the filming of *Romeo*

and Juliet, with Leslie Howard and John Barrymore going over their parts. Oliver Messel told me he had been there for months as a decorator and costume designer for *Romeo and Juliet*, and that most of the time he was merely waiting about, although he was being paid a very high fee. Looking at some of the masks he was making, I was reminded of a suggestion I made some time ago regarding historical characters on the screen. To my mind otherwise perfect representations were ruined by absurd casting of types. Henry VIII, Queen Elizabeth, Mary Queen of Scots, and many another well-known character are made to look ridiculous, while a silent film, with portrait masks, would bring back the past in a more dignified manner than any other means could approach. I feel sure that some producer will one day see there is something in the idea, and go back to the Greeks. When I suggested this it was pointed out that the number of people who were familiar with the features of historical personages were few compared with those familiar with the stars. The latest absurdity of representing an historical character on the screen is that of Clark Gable as Charles Stewart Parnell. Nothing could be more disconcerting to anyone who knew Parnell than to see and hear the travesty of a square-faced athlete with side whiskers and beetling brows representing the long ascetic features of one of the most cool and reserved of men. I could not sit it out. I could not get Thalberg to see that a perfect mask of, say, Queen Elizabeth's features as we know them, with a dignified, aloof expression, in a silent film going through her part in pantomime, would be so much more impressive and mysterious than any words, and would convey to the audience the feeling that the Queen was in another world remote from this. I mention Queen Elizabeth because of a remarkable mask I saw of her by Oliver Messel, so realistic as to be startling.

It was very difficult to find out what was going to take place on any of the sets at a given time. I was told, for instance, that the fight between the Capulets and Montagues would be shot in a couple of days. I spent two days painting the square of Verona ready for the event and hurried back the next morning expecting to get a blaze of colorful Florentine costumes, only to be told that the scene was postponed indefinitely. The balcony and the garden scenes were to be enacted next. I got the set ready painted, except for the lighting, which was to be turned on for me for half an hour only, because of the cost (the first indication of economy hinted at). When I asked for it I found that thirty-two electricians were necessary to work the lights, and they could not be spared for the moment. Next came the tomb scene. I was assured that I would get the three clear days they were devoting to the shooting. I spent the first day on the background and the details of the sarcophagus, which was being decorated by Messel. They told me that Miss Norma Shearer, as Juliet, was coming to pose, but that I should not be able to paint her as she was diffident about being looked at while being shot, and a screen had to be put up. It was not what I had come for. When she arrived I asked her if this was true; she said "Yes." I explained to her that Romeo without Juliet might not be understood, so she very kindly said she would see what she could do. The screen was taken away and I had the privilege of trying to paint her under varying lights, with Romeo first on one side and then on the other. When she had finished she came over to me, smiling. "You see what I was able to do for you." I thanked her, and as there were two clear days ahead I went home with a feeling that I saw something possible. To save the trouble of packing and unpacking my things I left them standing. Next morning the tomb, my painting outfit, and every vestige of the very elaborate scene had been cleared away, leaving a great empty studio in semidarkness. No one knew where my stuff had gone to, but some time afterwards the man who removed it was found and my unfinished work returned to me. I saw that I was beaten; there were so many cooks and I never saw the chef, who, I was told before leaving, was the Finance Committee, and I can well believe it, in view of the millions of dollars lavishly thrown about. No expense was spared, the question of a return for the outlay did not enter if the publicity was good.

Every day I was at the M-G-M Studios I joined the crowd in the large dining room — a kind of canteen — at luncheon time, and a picturesque crowd it was, mostly in costume of some period or other from *Romeo and Juliet* down to the present day. Sprinkled amongst them were people like myself in mufti — scenic artists, writers, and such like. The great stars and directors had a kind of officers' mess alone and did not mix with the crowd. Many of the faces were so familiar that I found myself throwing smiles and friendly nods to people who did not know me from Adam. Most of them seemed used to such attentions and returned the compliment by smiling back.

The one man I remember with a certain amount of pleasure and sympathy, who did his best for me, was George Cukor, who directed *Romeo and Juliet*. If ever I have seen patience personified it was by him. Working from early morn to dewy eve on raw material in every shape and form, from the pampered stars to the stupid extras that go to make a picture, never for a moment did he lose his temper or show signs of fatigue. When everyone else was dead-beat and believed that at last the scene was perfect, with the sweetest smile and the most charming manner imaginable he would say, "Now, ladies and gentlemen, we'll have just one more go to-morrow morning at eight, please."

Had I given myself three years instead of three weeks I might have made history, but I had not the time to spare for a new venture, in my eighties. According to their lights, people could not have been more considerate and obliging. Practically everything was placed at my disposal – except what I wanted, and that was to know what was going to take place and when. The waiting about was too much for me. On looking back I can see how stupid I was in attempting to compete with the camera, in spite of the protestations I had made to the contrary. Instead of looking at the detail I should have looked at it as a whole, as Turner would have done, conveying the strange lighting effects and mysterious forms; or I should have painted disconnected parts and joined them up on one canvas irrespective of apparent design – just as film pictures in the making. Another of my mistakes and missed opportunities.

XX

THE HOUSE BUILT ON SAND

My time at Hollywood was made a great deal more comfortable than it might have been owing to the hospitality of my friend Gordon Coutts, who had thrown open to me a most wonderful retreat of his at Palm Springs, only one hundred miles from Hollywood – which in America means "round the corner." It has the most perfect winter climate that I know, but it has two drawbacks for the painter: from April onwards the heat is excessive, and the light is blinding, which makes it necessary to wear smoked glasses the greater part of the day. It was practically a nudist colony; even old women and men wandered about wearing next to nothing. I took out a couple of models and piles of organdie and muslin dresses, but they looked so out of place that I painted my granddaughter Diana and a friend, Lillian Millar, sun-bathing.

Some years previously I had received a letter asking me if I recalled a boy called "Gordy" thirty years ago, and some kindness I had shown him which he always remembered. I could not recall either Gordy or the kindness. He went on to say that he had followed my progress through life and possessed every reproduction of my work which he could get hold of. He was coming to London to settle down as a portrait painter himself.

He came, but his health could not stand the climate. Later he wrote from California saying that since seeing me in London he had traveled far in search of health, had got married, and had lived in San Francisco until the earthquake came, when he and his wife had escaped injury but lost practically everything they possessed. He had wandered about picking up odd jobs and then gone to Morocco, leaving his wife in America. He regretted having saved her life in the earthquake – he had pushed her aside as a wall crashed – for she had behaved so badly since, finally going to Reno to take divorce proceedings against him. This caused him to return to contest the action, unsuccessfully and expensively. Now, however, he was married to a beautiful girl, an American Bohemian, who was studying to sing in Grand Opera. He had built himself a Moorish house more suited to the climate than any other type and making a really marvelous winter retreat. Wouldn't I come? I eventually took advantage of this when I made that visit to Hollywood which I have already described.

Gordon Coutts was a man of extraordinary will power. His father, I was told, had been a professional boxer, and the son from time to time gave amateur exhibitions in the noble art. He was born in Aberdeen, and was proud of his country and of his physical strength, which he did not fail to demonstrate when occasion arose. But when I saw him in California he was a poor weak invalid in a much-heated studio, unable to breathe anything but its vitiated air. I could only stay in it by sitting near the open door, causing him much discomfort which he tried to hide without complaint, being anxious for me to remain as long as he could stand the cold air coming in and I the foul air going out.

He held very pronounced views on art and artists in general, and contempt for what surrounded him in California. He seemed to be gasping for companionship and sympathy. He had an absorbing passion for Scotland and anyone associated with it, especially if that person happened to be a painter — that and the good turn I had done him had made him my friend. When he chose he had great charm, and many enthusiastic friends, male and female, only saw him from that angle. If he was a despot in his home they did not blame him. He forbade his wife and children to have any truck with her relatives, treating her sister as a kind of charwoman whom he tolerated so long as she did the work and kept out of sight. Still, he was everything to Gertrude, there was no sacrifice she would not make to please him, and yet he was so jealous that he could not bear to have her out of his sight. Even when she went to the village for the day's marketing he was on pins and needles until her return, when he would cross-question her as to whom she had met and what she had said, upbraiding and accusing until he brought tears. Once in a while her gypsy blood would boil up; there would be a battle, and she would chase him round the house with a knife after the manner of D. H. Lawrence and his wife.

He did not recover his health. When he lay dying

he said, "Gertrude, send for John Lavery." Perhaps in remorse he saw how intolerant he had been, and that someone must be with her. After his death she was dazed and wandered about demented for weeks, his spirit haunting her night and day until she could no longer stand it. Then she wrote telling me of his dying wish, and speaking of the peace and beauty of her place so far away from the worries of the world I lived in.

I am not going to air my troubles in public, as in any case I am usually so occupied with work that nothing else matters. It is true that, to a certain extent, the sufferings of others reach me, so that when Eileen and Hazel, for some reason known to the Divine Power, were made to suffer many months in agony I had an acute form of remorse afterwards. This caused me to bury myself in my painting until I was aroused to the fact that I was alone and being slowly led into a new life, opening up a vista of responsibilities I had no mind to face. So much was I averse to it that I was prepared to throw up everything and return to the happiest days of my existence – the life of an irresponsible Bohemian. This was the state of mind I was in when the letter came from Gertrude Coutts offering all that I had dreamed of. It came, surely, as the right word uttered at the right time. Even if somewhere in the background Mephistopheles was lurking, still, like Faust, I would make a new bid for life. I had lived one existence. It had come to an end. I would begin over – and even as an artist again. Many a time, tied down at Cromwell Place, I had longed for the freedom of the Bohemia I had known at first, and vainly hoped to recapture it one day. When a few years previously Hazel and I, after a terribly boring stay at the Riviera, had suddenly come upon a French colony of artists at Saint-Paul-du-Var, vividly reminding me of earlier days, we decided to go and live there for a bit; but after the luxury we had grown accustomed to, Hazel found that she could not rough it. She never really had Bohemian tastes.

But now came this invitation from across the ocean, and I saw a new chance to paint just as I pleased – with the bread-and-butter problem solved. The more I thought of this idea the more it grew within me until at last it obsessed me and took control. What was left for me at Cromwell Place? I had been there too long already, doing commissioned painting. I wanted to get away from it and strike out anew. I would end as I began – in freedom.

I accepted the invitation. In a mad rush I crossed the Atlantic and America, accompanied by my granddaughter Ann, and my secretary.

I could only faintly remember what Gertrude Coutts was like, other than as a downtrodden woman for whom, when I thought of her at all, I had a feeling of pity. I had a clear recollection of the evening at Palm Springs when Gordy came to the gate to bid me good-bye holding a handkerchief to his mouth to keep out the cold air – his wife well in the background. I now learnt that she had taken up motoring and she wanted to drive the whole way to New York to meet me! In the end she did drive three thousand miles to New Orleans, meeting us there. But it was not Mrs. Coutts who alighted from that car. Another woman stood before me, beautiful, wide-eyed, appealing — one who had evidently passed out of prison doors. She stood there offering me a new life in a land far away from convention. I was "possessed." The years fell from me; and, like a Faust who seemingly could dispense with the attentions of a Mephistopheles, I was a young man again with all the desires and aspirations of youth.

So we entered the car and drove southwards through the night, with the moon above and the smooth great road before us and cars flashing past at eighty miles an hour. As we neared our Promised Land, Gertrude lifted up her beautifully trained voice and sang the "Ave Maria." Suddenly she ceased singing and her voice was never heard again. There was a crash, and I found myself rising from the road — unhurt. Completely dazed, I began trying to lift a woman near the other car. Someone called out, "Don't touch her, she is dead." Then Ann's voice, saying, as she took my arm, "Katharine says you are to move away, there may be an explosion." Katharine was on her knees beside Gertrude. I heard her gasp, "I cannot breathe." Her back was broken. No way of relieving her. No doctor, only the white road and the wrecked cars. At last the ambulance. The drive the rest of the way to Palm Springs. I troubled over little things. Just as during the War one night at Hyde Park Corner, when Hazel was carried into St. George's Hospital, I went back to see if my late edition of the *Evening Standard* was in the shattered taxi, so now I sat waiting in the hospital at Palm Springs wondering if I had left my knife on the road, and if Gertrude, when she regained consciousness, would be angry when she saw her dress. But she never saw it; she died next day.

I had not allowed for the activities of Mephistopheles. I had not envisaged the extract from the *Palm Springs News* of December 20, 1937: "In the worst automobile accident in this area in two years, Mrs. Gertrude Coutts, the lovely widow of the famous painter Gordon Coutts, who died here less than a year ago, succumbed on Monday afternoon at two o'clock at the Reid Hospital owing to the terrible injuries received in the crash. . . . By a miracle Sir John Lavery, the British painter, his granddaughter, the Hon. Ann Forbes-Sempill, and his secretary, Miss Katharine FitzGerald, all of whom were riding in the Coutts machine, escaped injury."

I had built my house upon sand.

APPENDIX

PICTURES IN PUBLIC GALLERIES
1888–1939

NOTE. – The name of the model is underneath the title of the picture.

ENGLAND AND WALES

1903	THE MAYOR OF MORLEY *(Presented to the Gallery)*	Corporation of Morley Gallery
1905	THE LADY IN A GREEN COAT Frl. Mary Auras	Bradford
1906	VIOLET AND GOLD	Manchester
1907	RT. HON. WILLIAM KENDRICK	Birmingham
1909	TANGIER, EVENING Aïda	Birmingham
1913	THE ROYAL GROUP *(Presented by Hugh Spottiswoode, Esq.)*	National Portrait Gallery
1913–37	AUGUSTE RODIN	Victoria and Albert Museum
1916	ANNA PAVLOVA. LA MORT DU CYGNE *(Presented to Gallery by the International Society)*	Tate Gallery
1918	JAMES FITZMAURICE KELLY *(Presented to the Gallery)*	National Portrait Gallery

1920	COLLECTION OF 70 PICTURES	War Museum
1921	HAZEL IN ROSE AND GOLD	Liverpool
1921	THE VANDYKE ROOM AT WILTON (*Diploma Picture*)	Diploma Gallery, R.A.
1923	THE GOLF COURSE, NORTH BERWICK (*Presented by Lord Duveen*)	Tate Gallery
1924	STUDIES IN THE HOUSE OF LORDS	FitzWilliam Museum, Cambridge
1928	STATE OPENING OF THE NEW WING OF THE TATE GALLERY (*Presented by Lord Duveen*)	Tate Gallery
1930	THE CHESS PLAYERS The Hon. Margaret and Rosemary Scott-Ellis	Tate Gallery
1932	LADY LAVERY IN A MIRROR (*Presented by Lady Cunard*)	Guildhall Gallery
1936	SCHOOLING THE PONY Alice	Rochdale
1937	AUGUSTE RODIN	Removed to Tate Gallery
1938	RT. HON. J. RAMSAY MACDONALD, M.P.	National Portrait Gallery
1938	RT. HON. DAVID LLOYD GEORGE, M.P.	National Gallery of Wales

PICTURES IN PUBLIC GALLERIES

SCOTLAND

1888	STATE VISIT OF QUEEN VICTORIA TO GLASGOW *(Painted for the Executive Council of the Glasgow Exhibition)*	Corporation Gallery, Glasgow
1896	THE ROCKING CHAIR Mrs. Christie-Smith *(Diploma Picture)*	Edinburgh Diploma Gallery
1902	SHIPBUILDING (MURAL)	Banqueting Hall, Glasgow
1906	R. B. CUNNINGHAME GRAHAM	Glasgow
1913	CURLING	Scottish Modern Arts Association
1914	MRS. FITZROY BELL *(Bequeathed by Mrs. Fitzroy Bell)*	Glasgow
1915	FIRST WOUNDED IN LONDON HOSPITAL	Dundee
1916	MRS. R. B. CUNNINGHAME GRAHAM *(Presented by R. B. Cunninghame Graham)*	Glasgow
1918	SHIPBUILDING (SKETCH)	Glasgow
1919	A TENNIS PARTY Miss MacBride *(Bought from the Neue Pinakothek, Munich)*	Aberdeen
1922	VISCOUNT MORLEY ADDRESSING THE HOUSE OF LORDS	Glasgow
1924	ANNA PAVLOVA AS A BACCHANTE *(Presented by Nicol Paton Brown)*	Glasgow

1925	MISS MARY BURRELL (*Presented by Sir William Burrell*)	Glasgow
1930	RAMSAY MACDONALD ADDRESSING THE HOUSE OF COMMONS	Glasgow
1930	STEPHEN DONOGHUE IN THE KING'S COLOURS	Edinburgh
1930	SIR JAMES WATSON STEWART, BART. (*Painted for the Corporation of Glasgow*)	Glasgow
1935	A RALLY, 1885 (WATER COLOR) Miss MacBride	Glasgow
1935	115 STUDIES FOR THE STATE VISIT OF QUEEN VICTORIA TO GLASGOW	Glasgow
1935	MAIDENHEAD REGATTA	Glasgow
1937	SIR JAMES BARRIE, O.M.	National Portrait Gallery, Edinburgh
1937	EPSOM DOWNS	Greenock

IRELAND

1904	RT. HON. W. E. H. LECKY	National Gallery, Dublin
1914	DOCTOR SIGERSON	National Gallery, Dublin
1914	DORA SIGERSON SHORTER (*Presented by Clement Shorter*)	National Gallery, Dublin
1923	THE RED ROSE Hazel	Cork
1923	REQUIEM MASS FOR THE LORD MAYOR OF CORK	

	AT SOUTHWARK CATHEDRAL (STUDY) *(Presented to the Gallery)*	Cork
1924	THE LADY MAYORESS OF CORK *(Presented to the Gallery)*	Cork
1929	COLLECTION OF PAINTINGS	Municipal Gallery, Belfast

1. MOST REV. DR. CHARLES D'ARCY, ARCHBISHOP OF ARMAGH AND PRIMATE OF ALL IRELAND, 1928
2. RT. REV. DR. CHARLES T. P. GRIERSON, BISHOP OF CONNOR AND DOWN AND DRONMORE, 1928
3. MICHAEL CARDINAL LOGUE, PRIMATE OF ALL IRELAND, 1920
4. JOSEPH MACRORY, D.D., 1928
5. RT. HON. WILLIAM HUGH O'NEILL, D.L., 1ST SPEAKER OF THE HOUSE OF COMMONS, N.I., 1923
6. LORD CARSON, P.C., 1921
7. EILEEN, IN PRIMROSE YELLOW, 1926
8. SELF-PORTRAIT, 1928
9. THE DAYLIGHT RAID FROM MY STUDIO WINDOW, 1917
   Hazel
10. RT. HON. VISCOUNT CRAIGAVON, 1923
11. THE MARQUIS OF DUFFERIN AND AVA, D.S.O., 1923
12. THE MARQUIS OF LONDONDERRY, K.G., 1924
13. TANGIER BAY, SUNSHINE, 1920
14. SUMMER (THE RED HAMMOCK)
    Hazel

15. Eileen and Ann, 1923
16. Spring, 1921
17. Switzerland in Winter, 1913
18. The British Legation, Tangier, 1910
    Eileen and Sir Reginald Lister
19. The Mother, 1908
    Eileen
20. The Walls of Marakesh, 1920
21. The Cherry Tree, 1884
    Peasants
22. The Bridge at Grès, 1897
23. Twilight. The Lake at Geneva, 1924
24. Tangier Bay. Rain, 1910
25. Rt. Hon. Sir Edward M. Archdale, D.L., M.P., 1928
26. 12th July in Portadown, 1928
27. Joseph Devlin, Esq., M.P., 1928
28. Sir Joseph Davison, M.P., 1928
29. Lady Lavery, 1926
30. Study for the Royal Group in National Portrait Gallery, London, 1913
31. The Amazon
    Eileen
32. The Lady in Black
    Mrs. Treavor
33. London Hospital, 1914
    (*Lent by Mrs. Malcolm Mercer*)

1934	The Silver Casket	Queen's University, Belfast
1935	The Blessing of the Colours (Study)	Cork
1935	Collection of Paintings	Municipal Gallery, Dublin

1. John Lavery, by Hazel Lavery
2. Timothy O'Healy

PICTURES IN PUBLIC GALLERIES

3. Arthur Griffith
4. Michael Collins
5. E. S. O. Barton
6. Robert Barton
7. Gavan Duffy
8. David Lloyd George, M.P.
9. The Earl of Birkenhead
10. Winston Churchill, M.P.
11. Sir Austen Chamberlain, M.P.
12. Major Compton Smith (Posthumous)
13. William Cosgrave
14. Archbishop Mannix
15. Kevin O'Higgins
16. Eamon de Valera
17. Michael Collins (Love of Ireland)
18. Hugh Nihill Kennedy
19. Sir Horace Plunkett
20. The Earl of Dunraven
21. Viscount Northcliffe
22. George Bernard Shaw
23. Shane Leslie
24. Pro Cathedral — Dublin, 1922
25. Southwark Cathedral — London, 1920
26. Court of Criminal Appeal (Study) — London, 1916
27. The First Irish Airwoman
28. Sir Alfred Cope
29. The Blessing of the Colours
30. Count John MacCormack and His Family
31. Hazel Lavery
32. St. Patrick's Purgatory
33. The Unfinished Harmony, 1934

34. IT IS FINISHED, JANUARY 4, 1935
MRS. LAVERY SKETCHING
(Presented by Hugh Lane)
LA DAME AUX PERLES
The Baroness von Höllrigl
(Presented by Hugh Lane)
THE WHARF, SUTTON COURTENAY
Elizabeth Asquith, Violet and Stephen McKenna
(Presented by Count John MacCormack)

1937	STARS IN SUNLIGHT (MAUREEN O'SULLIVAN AND LORETTA YOUNG)	Limerick

AUSTRALIA

1908	WHITE FEATHERS Nora Johnson	Sydney
1913	IN MOROCCO Hazel, Alice, and Ben Ali	Adelaide
1919	BASQUE COUNTRY	New South Wales

CANADA

1910	MARY IN GREEN Frl. Mary Auras	Ottawa
1913	PRINCESS PATRICIA OF CONNAUGHT	Toronto

INDIA

1933	LADY TATA *(Presented by Mr. Mehta)*	Bombay Museum

PICTURES IN PUBLIC GALLERIES

AMERICA

1897	The Bridge at Grès (A Passing Salute)	Pittsburgh
1899	A Garden in France Madame Heseltine	Philadelphia
1911	Evening, Tangier	Chicago
1922	Lady Diana Cooper (The Invalid) With Hazel and Viscountess de Janze	Pittsburgh
1925	Lady Diana Cooper	Brooklyn
1926	Wimborne House (Interior)	Harrisburg
1932	Mrs. Alma de Botteville Spreckles	Legion of Honor Gallery, San Francisco
1932	Study for Their Majesties' Court *(Presented by Mrs. Spreckles)*	Legion of Honor Gallery, San Francisco
1939	Wilfred Meynell	Francis Thompson Memorial Library, Boston
1939	Coventry Patmore (Posthumous)	Francis Thompson Memorial Library, Boston

SOUTH AMERICA

1910	The Blonde Miss Neville	Buenos Aires
1911	Miss Lily Elsie	Santiago, Chile
1933	R. B. Cunninghame Graham on Pampa *(Presented by R. B. Cunninghame Graham)*	Buenos Aires

SOUTH AFRICA

1903	MARY WITH ROSES Frl. Mary Auras *(Presented by Hugh Lane)*	Johannesburg

FRANCE

1900	PÈRE ET FILLE John Lavery and Eileen	Luxembourg (Later Jeu de Paume)
1903	SUMMER	Musée Rodin
1903	EILEEN Lavery	Musée Rodin
1903	IDONIA La Primaudye	Musée Rodin
1904	PRINTEMPS Frl. Mary Auras	Luxembourg (Later Jeu de Paume)

GERMANY

1901–18	A TENNIS PARTY Miss MacBride *(Purchased by Gallery. Sold Aberdeen, 1918)*	Neue Pinakothek, Munich
1904	LADY IN BLACK Esther MacLaren	Kaiser Friedrich Museum, Berlin
1904	A Modern Venus Frl. Marta Heydorn	Leipzig
1904	THE GREEN HAMMOCK Nora Johnson	Mannheim
1904	LANDSCAPE	Stuttgart

ITALY

1899	MRS. LAURIE AND EDWIN	Venice

PICTURES IN PUBLIC GALLERIES

1906	SELF-PORTRAIT (*Commissioned by Gallery*)	Uffizi, Florence
1907	THE SOKO, TANGIER	Chamber of Commerce, Venice
1909	POLYMNIA Mary Delmar Morgan	Rome
1910	A LADY IN PINK Mary Delmar Morgan	Venice
1915	PRINCESS BIBESCO	Rome

BELGIUM

1899	NIGHT AFTER THE BATTLE OF LANGSIDE Bella Cullen	Brussels Museum
1900	LADY IN BLACK Thalia Tredwell	Brussels Museum

JANE LAVERY, MY SISTER, 1876

Made and printed in Great Britain

PIOUS REFLECTIONS, 1879

Made and printed in Great Britain

A TENNIS PARTY, 1884

DETAIL FROM ABOVE

Made and printed in Great Britain

THE DAWN AFTER THE BATTLE OF LANGSIDE, 1887

Made and printed in Great Britain

STATE VISIT OF QUEEN VICTORIA TO GLASGOW, 1888

STUDY OF QUEEN VICTORIA FOR ABOVE

Made and printed in Great Britain

STUDY OF PRINCESS ALIX OF HESSE
(LAST EMPRESS OF RUSSIA), 1888

Made and printed in Great Britain

KATHLEEN (THE FLOWER GIRL), 1889

Made and printed in Great Britain

THE MODEL, 1896

PERE ET FILLE, 1897

Made and printed in Great Britain

R. B. CUNNINGHAME GRAHAM ON PAMPA, 1898

MRS. BROWN POTTER, 1901

Made and printed in Great Britain

A MOORISH HAREM, 1907

THE BLACK CAP (MR. JUSTICE DARLING), 1907

Made and printed in Great Britain

SELF-PORTRAIT (UFFIZI GALLERY), 1910

MY STUDIO; HAZEL, EILEEN, ALICE AND AIDA, 1911

Made and printed in Great Britain

PAVLOVA AS "THE DYING SWAN," 1911

Made and printed in Great Britain

WILLIAM PATRICK WHYTE, 1912

Made and printed in Great Britain

KING GEORGE V, QUEEN MARY, THE PRINCE OF WALES,
PRINCESS MARY, 1913

Made and printed in Great Britain

JAPANESE SWITZERLAND (HAZEL AND ALICE), 1913

Made and printed in Great Britain

FIRST WOUNDED, LONDON HOSPITAL, AUGUST, 1914

Made and printed in Great Britain

JOHN LAVERY BY WINSTON CHURCHILL, 1915

WINSTON CHURCHILL, BY JOHN LAVERY, 1915

Made and printed in Great Britain

THE COURT OF CRIMINAL APPEAL—HIGH TREASON TRIAL, 1916

Made and printed in Great Britain

THE ARRIVAL OF THE GERMAN DELEGATES, ON H.M.S. QUEEN ELIZABETH, 15th NOVEMBER, 1918

Made and printed in Great Britain

THE MARQUIS OF LONDONDERRY, K.G., 1919

Made and printed in Great Britain

EAMON DE VALERA, 1921

SIR EDWARD CARSON, 1916

Made and printed in Great Britain

WILLIAM COSGRAVE, 1923

KEVIN O'HIGGINS, 1921

Made and printed in Great Britain

HAZEL; PORTRAIT IN A MIRROR, 1922

Made and printed in Great Britain

WEDDING PROCESSION OF PRINCESS MARY, IN GREEN PARK, 1922

Made and printed in Great Britain

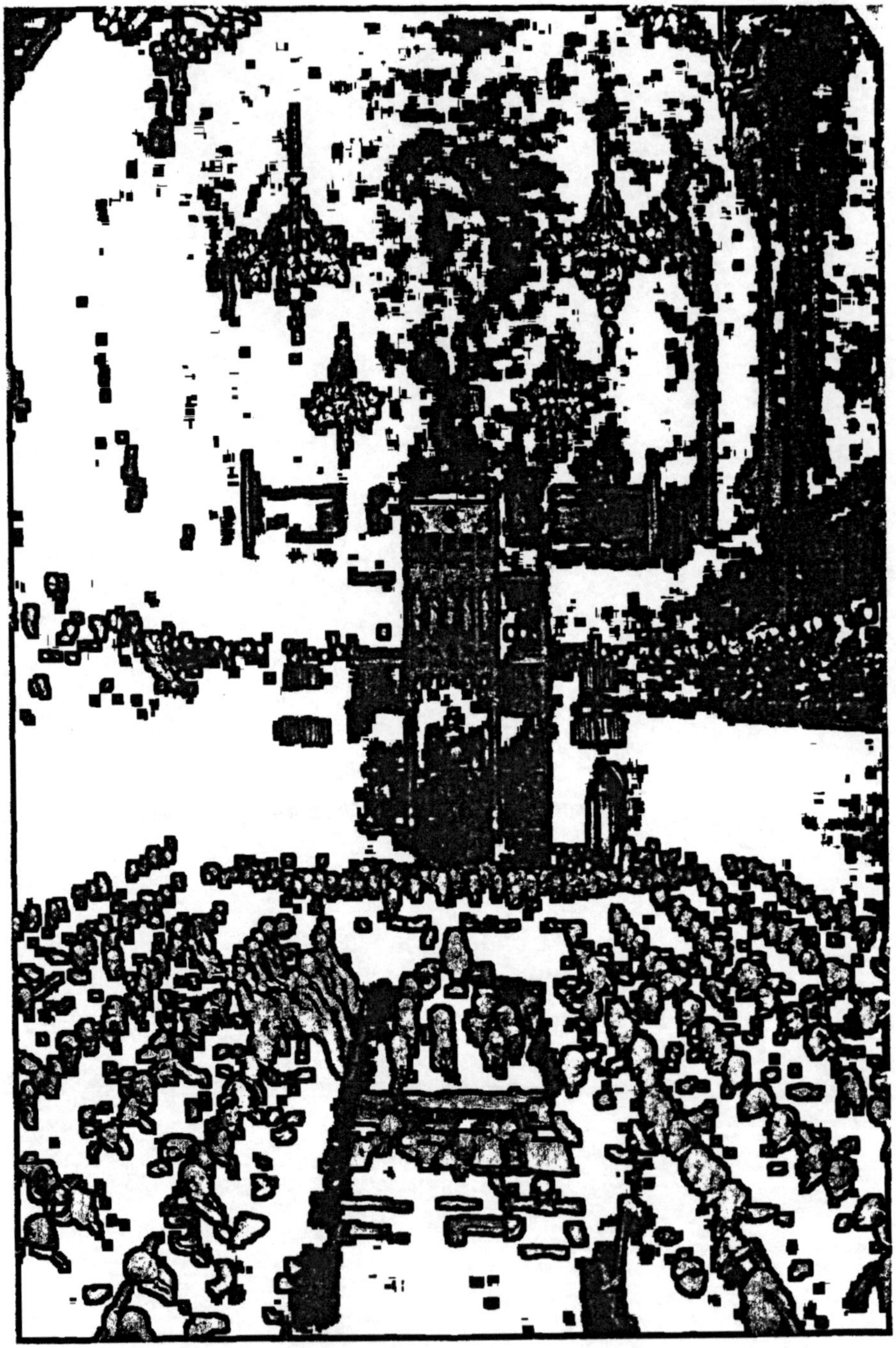

VISCOUNT MORLEY MOVING THE ADDRESS ON THE IRISH TREATY IN THE HOUSE OF LORDS, 1922

Made and printed in Great Britain

ALICE, 1922

Made and printed in Great Britain

RAMSAY MACDONALD ADDRESSING THE HOUSE OF COMMONS FIRST LABOUR GOVERNMENT, 1923

Made and printed in Great Britain

STEPHEN DONOGHUE IN THE
KING'S COLOURS, 1923

Made and printed in Great Britain

EILEEN AND ANN, 1923

Made and printed in Great Britain

IRISH BANK NOTE, 1923

DETAIL OF HEAD

Made and printed in Great Britain

THE MARCHIONESS OF LONDONDERRY, AND MAIRI, 1923

Made and printed in Great Britain

GEORGE BERNARD SHAW, BY HAZEL LAVERY, 1925

Made and printed in Great Britain

EMERALD LADY CUNARD AND GEORGE MOORE, 1925

Made and printed in Great Britain

MARY BORDEN AND HER FAMILY AT BISHAM ABBEY, 1926

Made and printed in Great Britain

ST PATRICK'S PURGATORY, 1930

Made and printed in Great Britain

ON HAMPSTEAD HEATH, 1930

Made and printed in Great Britain

THEIR MAJESTIES' COURT, 1932

Made and printed in Great Britain

JAMES MAXTON, M.P., 1933

Made and printed in Great Britain

THE PRIME MINISTER AT LOSSIEMOUTH, 1933

Made and printed in Great Britain

THE COUNTESS OF OXFORD AND ASQUITH, 1934

Made and printed in Great Britain

DAVID LLOYD GEORGE, 1935

Made and printed in Great Britain

SHIRLEY TEMPLE AND THE PAINTER, 1936

Made and printed in Great Britain

PICCADILLY, 12th MAY, 1937

Made and printed in Great Britain

SUNBATHERS (DIANA AND LILLIAN WITH MARY COUTTS), 1937

Made and printed in Great Britain

JOHN MASEFIELD, READING THE PAINTER'S MS., 1937

Made and printed in Great Britain

LILLIAN AT RANELAGH, 1936

Made and printed in Great Britain

KATHARINE FITZGERALD, 1939

Made and printed in Great Britain

Lightning Source UK Ltd.
Milton Keynes UK
UKOW02f1051220514

232123UK00001B/52/P